Triumph in death

The story of the Malagasy martyrs

F.G. Smith

Foreword by J. Elwyn Davies

EVANGELICAL PRESS
16/18 High Street, Welwyn, Hertfordshire, AL6 9EQ, England

© Evangelical Press 1987

First published 1987

ISBN 0 85234 242 X

British Library Cataloguing in Publication Data

Smith, F.G.
    Triumph in death: the story of the Malagasy martyrs.
    1. Christian martyrs-Madagascar-History-19th century
    I. Title
    272'.9 BR1608.M3

    ISBN 0 85234 242 X

Unless otherwise indicated, all Scripture references are taken from the New International Version, Hodder and Stoughton, 1984.

Illustrations
Line drawings are reproduced from the following works:
J.J. Freeman & D. Johns, *A Narrative of the Persecution of Christians in Madagascar*, John Snow, London, 1840
W. Ellis, *Three Visits to Madagascar*, John Murray, London, 1858.
Photographs are reproduced by courtesy of Paul Appéré

Typeset by Alan Sutton Publishing, Gloucester
Printed in Great Britain by the Bath Press, Avon.

Contents

Foreword	5
Introduction	9
The Malagasy language	13
1 The gospel comes to Madagascar	15
2 Madagascar as it was	23
3 David Jones begins his work	31
4 A new queen	39
5 The blow falls	51
6 The translation of the Bible	59
7 The storm breaks out afresh	69
8 The persecution continues	81
9 Andriambelo	91
10 Closing years of the persecution	99
11 The sun shines again	107
12 The ongoing story	115
Notes	119
Glossary	121
Chronology of important events	125
Bibliography	127

Foreword

Moments of bidding farewell to one's friends can be memorable, particularly when great distances are involved. Two such partings, involving the author of this book, come to mind as I welcome the opportunity of commending his most valuable account of the founding of the Christian church in Madagascar.

The first occurred outside his home in Sydney, New South Wales. As we were about to leave, to our utter astonishment, both he and his wife, in broad Australian accents, broke into a hearty and most convincing rendering of a well-known Welsh children's ditty. It had been drilled into them, it seems, by a Welsh-speaking missionary colleague during their years of service together in Madagascar. It was, we thought, a salutary reminder of the tremendous contribution missionaries from Wales had made to the work of God in that distant land.

For the sake of their children's education the author and his wife had been obliged to leave Madagascar in 1964 after fourteen years of faithful service. It was evident, however, that their labours in that country and, in particular, their respect for the story of its martyrs of barely a century before had left an indelible impression upon them. It therefore came as no surprise to us to learn some time later that this book was in preparation.

Our second parting was no less memorable. It was on a bleak November morning in 1986. This time they were about to leave our home in South Wales to realize a long-standing ambition: they were to visit the site of the Neuaddlwyd

School in West Wales, where the pioneer missionaries whose story is related in this book received their early education and, more significantly still, their call to the mission-field. No ditties were sung on this occasion, but there was a song of rejoicing in all our hearts. By a remarkable providence another missionary friend, whose home today is not many miles from the neighbourhood of that old school, had called at our home the previous day to show slides of the work of God in Madagascar which he had just witnessed, and to which he hoped to return shortly. (It is not without significance that the royalties from the sale of this book will help in furthering the work of two missionaries with strong Australian and Welsh links who are serving in Madagascar today – John Williams and his wife Catherine.)

Australia . . . Madagascar . . . Wales – why is it important that Christians in all these countries, and indeed throughout the world, should be reminded of the epic story of the Malagasy church and its heroic martyrs? Many reasons could be given. No higher tribute could be paid to the crucial importance of the Word of God and its ability to succour and support Christians, particularly in times of trial and affliction, than is found within the pages of this book. Then there is the outstanding courage of the Malagasy martyrs, and the staggering contrast between the way they conducted themselves and the behaviour of their persecutors, many of whom were their blood-relations. Nowhere could we hope to find a more telling testimony to the miracle of regeneration and the subsequent growth in spiritual stature of new men and women than is to be found in the history of this people. Nothing but the grace of almighty God could have brought about such a transformation. Or again, we could be forgiven for thinking that here is singular evidence indeed of the supreme wisdom of the Lord of the church as he governs his people. Why were Welsh-speaking missionaries called upon to play such a crucial role in establishing the Malagasy alphabet, transcribing its language and translating the Scriptures into that language, all within the space of fifteen years? (Wales's contribution to the missionary movement of the nineteenth century, although not insignificant, could hardly be called momentous.) Could it be the fact that their native Welsh tongue, being, unlike English, a phonetic language, provided them with the exact discipline which they needed for their task?

But there is one reason which stands supreme. The Scriptures teach us that as Christians we are caught up in a struggle of horrendous proportions with the powers of darkness. This is a truth which we forget at our peril, for he who 'deceives the whole world' is as actively engaged today as ever he was, making war with 'the rest of [the] offspring, those who obey God's commandments and hold to the testimony of Jesus'. To forget this awesome power struggle, as we think of many parts of our world where today there is open persecution of Christians, sometimes by the state itself, is to fly in the face of biblical truth. To forget it, when we ourselves are involved in identical, if subtler, forms of this same warfare, is to offer ourselves and each other as innocent prey to the enemy. This book brings us a compelling reminder of this other dimension – the world of close and sometimes fatal encounters with the enemy of our souls. As it tells the story of a humble, unsophisticated body of first-generation Christians trusting their God, feeding avidly upon his Word and, amidst the most terrible dangers to life and limb, enjoying his presence, their faces often resplendent with his glory, may it strengthen us for the battle and convince us too that 'The one who is in you is greater than the one who is in the world.'

J. Elwyn Davies

Introduction

Why tell this story? What relevance has this account of nineteenth-century persecution in a little-known part of the world for twentieth-century Christians? Most of the material in this book has been drawn from books produced in the last century, which are now long out of print. Have these old volumes, these events of long ago, even if retold in today's language, anything to say to the Christians of this generation? I am convinced that the answer is 'Yes', that this story of heroism and faith should not be allowed to be forgotten.

In the first place these Malagasy Christians whose sufferings are recounted in these pages are fellow Christians with us. They are a part of the body of Christ, and we and they by his grace will share in the glories of the hereafter. They have indeed already entered into blessedness, for by faith they endured to the end, 'looking forward to the city with foundations, whose architect and builder is God' (Heb. 11:10). They are not an obscure and forgotten people of no interest to us. The faith they professed is the same faith that we hold today. They sealed their testimony with their blood, proving in their own selves the power of their Lord.

Secondly, the persecution of the people of God is not a strange phenomenon which we can dismiss as irrelevant. Persecution for the faith began in New Testament times and even earlier. The stoning of Stephen, the imprisonment of the apostles, the death of James and the deliverance of Peter have been repeated again and again throughout the Christian era, and never more so than in this present century. Trial and suffering are of the very essence of

Christianity. We need to be aware of this, and we need to know how our suffering brethren faced their persecutors and how they fared. Christ our Saviour suffered for us; it is to be expected that his people may be called upon to suffer for him. Peter expressed it clearly in his first letter, saying, 'Dear friends, do not be surprised at the painful trial you are suffering, as though something strange were happening to you. But rejoice that you participate in the sufferings of Christ' (1 Peter 4:12–13).

There is a third reason why this account is of value to us today, and why it should not be forgotten. It is an example and an out-working of the age-long conflict between good and evil, between Christ and his church on the one hand and Satan and his forces on the other. The power behind Ránaválona and her ministers was the power of Satan himself. From the time of Cain and his brother Abel until Christ returns in glory the story is one. Christ has established a church and has declared that the gates of Hades will not overcome it. Cain killed his brother Abel; Pharaoh killed all the male Israelite children in Egypt; Athaliah destroyed the whole royal family in Jerusalem, and Haman plotted to destroy all the Jews in Persia and Media, to cite just a few examples. Another son was raised up in place of Abel. Moses was preserved and grew up to deliver his people. Josiah was hidden and so the royal family was not wiped out. Christ would still be born of the line of David. Haman's wicked plot was discovered and foiled and God's people were preserved. The New Testament opens with the massacre of the children of Bethlehem, with the express purpose of destroying the Son of God before he could accomplish his redeeming work. Revelation chapter 12 sketches the full picture. When Christ the man-child was born, the dragon 'stood in front of the woman . . . so that he might devour her child'. He continues to this day to make war with the rest of her offspring (Rev. 12:17). Every act of oppression of God's people, every persecution of Christians, from the book of Acts until now, is part of the same great conflict. The devil is determined to destroy the church of Jesus Christ, but he is doomed to failure and to final defeat. If he failed in Madagascar, then he will fail anywhere.

On more than one occasion Queen Ranavalona and her

Introduction

ministers thought they had silenced the testimony of the Christians. But every time the futility of their efforts was manifested. The Malagasy are a people prone to fear, and they are more ready to voice their fears than are Europeans. But the Christians who went to their death showed no fear, to the constant amazement and consternation of their tormentors. They triumphed in the way they faced death, and had no Christian believer remained alive in Madagascar it would still have been a victory for the gospel.

But the gospel triumphed in another way as well. When the persecution began in 1835 there were 200 baptized believers and several hundred others who were also believers in Jesus Christ. Their numbers would not have exceeded 1000, and most of these would have been converts of less than three years' standing. During the twenty-six years of persecution the queen enslaved and punished some thousands of Christians. More than 200 were directly put to death by fire or sword. Many fled and were never heard of again. Large numbers were imprisoned or enslaved or banished to distant parts of the island. Many of these died as a result of their privations. Those who remained alive continued true to the faith, but not only so, others were constrained to join their company. In the year 1861, before the London Missionary Society had recommenced its work in Madagascar, the number of Christian believers was estimated to be 7000. This was not mere human perseverance; this was a demonstration of the power of Christ and of his gospel.

Everywhere today the church faces either persecution or compromise or coldness or contends with error within its ranks. Can it survive? When the Son of Man comes will he find faith on the earth? We may be sure he will. The church of Jesus Christ will survive, and more than survive – it will triumph. Christ will bring his people in from among every tribe, language and nation. The Christians of Madagascar had the Scriptures in their own language. That was the secret of their perseverance. They nourished their souls on the Word of God and were strong. In the Word they found the Christ and he did not fail nor forsake them in their hour of trial. The people of God today, in many trying and desperate situations, are finding the promises of God just as real and the power of Christ just as sustaining as did the Malagasy martyrs of the last century. That is the message of this story; may we heed it and take courage.

The Malagasy language

A few words of explanation may be helpful to enable the readers of this narrative to pronounce with some correctness the Malagasy words and names which have found their way into the story. The language of the Malagasy is a liquid, smooth-flowing language and there are in reality no 'tongue-twisters' in pronouncing any part of it. Here are a few simple rules which, if followed, will make it unnecessary to jump over words and names as they appear.

Vowels are pronounced approximately as follows:

    a as *a* in f*a*ther   = *fady* (taboo)
    e as *a* in l*a*te   = *tangéna*
    i as *ee* in m*ee*t   = *Ranivo*
    o as *oo* in t*oo*   = *Rakóto*

y represents the same sound as i, but is used only at the end of a word, e.g. *kabary*.

There are only two diphthongs in the language:
(1) *ai*, or *ay*, which are pronounced *i* as in m*i*ght, e.g., *lay* = a sail, or Ra*i*nitsiandavaka
(2) *ao* is pronounced *ow* as in n*ow*, e.g. Iz*ao*.
In all other cases, where two vowels are placed together both are pronounced,
    e.g. *Andriana* is *Án-drí-ana*
         Betsileo is *Bé-tsi-lé-o*.
But how does one pronounce these great long names? How does one begin to say, 'Rainitsiandavaka', for instance? The first thing to remember is that the language flows with a lilt and that there are fairly well-defined rules of accentuation.

i. The final *e* in a word is always accented, e.g. *manomé* = to give, or *dité* = tea. This determines the accent on any other syllables, so the first word must be *mánomé*.

ii. In most other words the accent is on the second-last syllable. So Andohalo is pronounced Án-do-hálo, and *kabary* is *ka-báry*.

iii. Words with weak endings, i.e. words ending in *na, ka,* or *tra* are accented on the third last or ante-penultimate syllable.

So Imerina is pronounced I-mér-i-na.

Ranavalona is pronounced Rá-na-vá-lo-na

Rainitsiandavaka is pronounced Rái-ni-tsí-an-dá-va-ka

So that is all there is to it! Remember that 'ai' is a diphthong, and that all the vowels are pronounced as above.

Martyr Memorial Church, Ambohipotsy

1.
The gospel comes to Madagascar

Thomas Phillips had a burden. His burden was for the island of Madagascar in the Indian Ocean. He had never been there, but he had read much about the great island and he was troubled. For here was a people without the light of the gospel of Jesus Christ. From all he had read of Madagascar, the words of Isaiah the prophet seemed aptly to describe that land and its people: 'See, darkness covers the earth and thick darkness is over the peoples' (Isa. 60:2). He longed to be able to change that picture, to bring about the change Isaiah predicted: 'But the Lord rises upon you and his glory appears over you.' But what could he do? He was too old to offer himself for missionary service. But if he could not go to Madagascar with the gospel, then who would?

His burden would not go away. Then one night he had a dream. He saw in his dream a beautiful island with high mountains and plains, and a savage people calling out, 'Come over and help us.' He felt certain, when he awoke, that his dream was of the island of Madagascar, of which he had already heard.

Thomas Phillips' trouble of heart should not surprise us. He was an ardent supporter of the newly formed London Missionary Society, and he had followed with much interest the beginnings of its work in the South Seas. But what of Madagascar? When would its turn come?

The Rev. Thomas Phillips was the principal of a school for preachers at Neuaddlwyd in South Wales. He decided to share his burden with the students in his college. He told them of Madagascar and of its need for the gospel, and then he put to them the simple question: 'Who will go as a missionary to Madagascar?' The challenge was sudden and unexpected, and for a few moments no one moved. Then one young man stood to his feet and said, 'I will go.' His name was David Jones. Then his friend and fellow student, Thomas Bevan, stood to his feet beside David.[1]

How did it come about that in this small college in South Wales in the year 1816 two young men should respond in such a way to such a challenge? Madagascar was almost on the other side of the world, its people practically unknown to the people of the British Isles. For answer we must look at the situation as it was then, in both Britain and Madagascar. In Britain the church was awaking from sleep. At the beginning of the eighteenth century spiritual life there had sunk to such a low ebb that someone once remarked that nobody ever spoke of Christianity except to scoff at it. Churches were empty and preaching was devoid of meaning. Gross doctrinal errors were propagated and 'enthusiasm' was regarded as being in the worst possible taste. But all this was changed by the preaching of George Whitefield and John Wesley and of others whom God raised up to labour alongside them. Within a generation a great change came over the whole country. Churches were filled again and Methodist societies sprang up in town and city.

Multitudes came under the sound of the gospel and great numbers of people in England and Wales were brought to faith in Jesus Christ.

In the mercy of God the Great Awakening was not of short duration. Christians were aroused to do something about the many social ills which disfigured the face of Britain. In addition, men began to lift up their eyes to lands beyond the seas. Through the voyages of Captain Cook the whole Pacific region had become known. Some saw only the noble savage in a blessed Arcadia, but the Christian church saw a people for whom Christ had died. India too was becoming better known, and though the East India Company forbad missionaries to enter its territory, the nearby Dutch concession provided a foothold for William Carey, founder of the Baptist Missionary Society. That society was born in 1792 and soon afterwards Carey, Marshman and Ward sailed for Calcutta. There they engaged in a prodigious activity of preaching, teaching and Bible translation.

Three years later, in 1795, the Missionary Society, soon to be called the London Missionary Society, was brought into being, with the object of taking 'the glorious gospel of blessed God to the heathen', as its original charter affirms. In the following year the *Duff* sailed to the South Seas with a party of missionaries. Within a few years there came into being another organization which was to be of immense value in this new missionary activity. That was the British and Foreign Bible Society, formed in March 1804 with the declared object of making the Bible available to every man in his own language and at a price he could afford to pay. There would soon be more than ample work for the Bible Society as it worked hand in hand with missionary societies throughout the world.

But what of Madagascar? The resources of the newly formed Missionary Society were concentrated almost exclusively in the South Seas and Southern Africa. But this was not to say that the society was unconcerned about other areas of the globe. Many places, including the island of Madagascar, were known to the directors of the society, but the way of advance into these other lands had not yet opened up.

There had been earlier attempts to evangelize and

Antananarivo - the capital of Madagascar

The gospel comes to Madagascar

colonize Madagascar, but these had not been crowned with any lasting success. The English, in the reign of Charles I (1618–1649), had their schemes for colonizing Madagascar, for propagating the Christian religion there and for enriching the coffers of the king by trade with what was thought to be a country of immense natural resources. Across the water in France the French Society of the Orient was formed in 1642 in the reign of Louis XIV and under the patronage of the immensely powerful Cardinal Richelieu. Great plans were laid for the colonization of Madagascar and for the conversion of its inhabitants to the Roman Catholic faith. But all of these efforts had ended in failure. The French made a further attempt in the 1760s to evangelize the Malagasy people, but again nothing permanent was accomplished. Madagascar was left to the pirates, who sallied forth from its bays and harbours to harry Indian Ocean shipping. Otherwise its ports were only staging posts for shipping to India and the Far East.

But now, with the dawn of the nineteenth century, there was a new kind of interest in Madagascar. It became the focus of attention of evangelical missionary societies. The thick darkness which had covered the island for so long was soon to be broken.

Van der Kemp, an officer of the Dutch Dragoons, was a man of many talents and great determination and possessed great intellectual gifts. But because of his notoriously fast life he was compelled to resign from his regiment. He undertook medical studies and qualified as a doctor. Soon afterwards he experienced a dramatic conversion. He was sent by the L.M.S. as a missionary to the Hottentots in South Africa and he arrived in Cape Town in 1797. Great was his love for the people among whom he laboured, but the island of Madagascar also captured his attention. He wrote repeatedly to the directors of the L.M.S. in London, drawing their attention to Madagascar as a field for their labours. He suggested Cape Town as a starting-point for a mission to the west coast in the region of the Bay of St Augustine. He even offered himself as a missionary to Madagascar if no one else was willing to go. But the heavy responsibilities of his own work in South Africa hindered him from making a start.

In 1810 Ile de France was captured by Britain during the Napoleonic wars and renamed Mauritius. The island is just a few hundred miles east of Madagascar. Van der Kemp saw it as another possible means of entry into Madagascar. But now he was held back by his own ill-health. He died in Cape Town in December 1811 without seeing his ambition realized.

Van der Kemp was not the only one to display an interest in Madagascar. As early as 1795 Captain Andrew Burns, a professional soldier, had presented a proposal to the (London) Missionary Society[2] that a mission should be begun in Madagascar. He wrote from first-hand experience, having spent about six weeks at the Bay of St Augustine. But Burns' proposal was not taken up at the time by the directors of the society.

Following the British annexation of Mauritius, Robert Farquhar was appointed governor. Mauritius depended heavily on Madagascar for supplies of slaves, as well as rice and cattle. The main point of contact was the port of Toamasina, or Tamatave, on the east coast. Although Van der Kemp did not live to take advantage of the opportunity offered of entry into Madagascar from Mauritius, the Missionary Society saw the possibilities, and in May 1814 the Rev. Jean le Brun, a native of Jersey, was sent to Mauritius. He was to begin a mission there or to explore the possibility of opening a work in Madagascar, as the Lord opened the way. In the event he remained in Mauritius and gave the long years of his life to the work there, including a fruitful ministry among the many Malagasy who had been brought to Mauritius as slaves. But he did not have the honour of bringing the gospel to the people of Madagascar in their own land.

That honour belonged to David Jones and Thomas Bevan. We take up again the story of these two young men from Wales who willingly offered themselves for the work of the Lord. They proceeded to Gosport in England for the completion of their training at the missionary college of the London Missionary Society. Then they returned to their home town in Wales. (David Jones had been born in Neuaddlywd in 1797 and Thomas Bevan in a village nearby two years earlier.) Their valedictory service was a most impressive occasion, attended by more than 5000 people. There was no building able to house them all and the service was held in the open air. No less than seven sermons were preached on that occasion. The whole proceedings were a source of strength and encouragement to the two young men.

The two young pioneers and their wives sailed from England in February 1818 and arrived in Mauritius in July of the same year. They found the colony of Mauritius in a ferment. Governor Farquhar had been invalided home and General Hall was in charge. Among other things General Hall seems to have broken off all contact between Mauritius and Madagascar. The two missionaries were regaled with tales of the ferocious and treacherous character of the Malagasy people and the wickedness of the slave traders.

They were not daunted, however, and the two men decided to make at once an exploratory visit to the east coast of Madagascar. They arrived in August 1818 and were warmly received by Bragg, the English trader, and by Jean René, the Malagasy chief at Toamasina. A school-house was built, and they soon had a group of Malagasy children learning to read. This beginning of the work was most encouraging. After a few weeks they returned to Mauritius in order to bring their families to Madagascar and so begin their work in earnest. The two women were not in good health, and also were in some distress on account of the attitude of some people in Mauritius, who found the idea of bringing the gospel to the Malagasy a cause of ribald mirth.

Soon Mrs Jones's health improved, so with her new-born baby she accompanied her husband to Toamasina. They were joyfully received by the pupils at the school and, indeed, by all the townspeople. The schoolchildren had been teaching others what they had learned so far and were eager to begin again at their lessons. But it was now November and the beginning of the wet season and the dreaded malarial fever began to take its toll. Within a short time all three of the newcomers were smitten by fever. Before the end of December first the baby and then Mrs Jones were called by God to himself. David himself was desperately ill. Meanwhile Thomas Bevan and his family set sail from Mauritius and arrived in Toamasina on 6 January

1819. They expected to find their colleagues alive and well and busy in the work, but, alas, they were greeted on arrival with the sad news of sickness and death.

When Thomas Bevan came into the house where his co-worker lay ill and near death, he voiced the thought that was in his mind: 'I shall certainly die,' he said, 'but you will recover and proceed with your work, and ultimately succeed in the mission.' And so it came about. Early in January 1919 both Thomas Bevan and his wife were stricken with fever. Within a fortnight their child was suddenly taken ill and died. Thomas Bevan died on 31 January and his wife three days later. So in less than a month David Jones found himself the sole survivor of a party of six. He managed to crawl, more dead than alive, on to a cattle boat, and returned to Mauritius, where he was nursed back to health. The rumour has persisted that the Malagasy fever was not the sole cause of these deaths. Poison has been suspected, for not all at Toamasina and in the district welcomed the new arrivals, particularly the slave traders. Even the English trader Bragg, who had been so helpful at the beginning, turned against David Jones. However, Jones had heard that King Radama had invited him to his capital and he determined to return. He had no intention of giving up his task, though it had been begun in sorrow and tears. He knew himself to be called of God and as soon as he had regained his health his eyes were turned once more towards the great island of Madagascar and its people.

Betsimasaraka mother and child and a Hova woman

2.
Madagascar as it was

The island of Madagascar seems first to have been made known to the people of Europe by the celebrated Venetian traveller, Marco Polo, towards the end of the thirteenth century. He reported the existence of a large African island which he named Madagascar or Magaster. The description he gives of the island, however, belongs more properly to parts of Africa.

The inhabitants did not use the name Madagascar, but called their island *Izao ambány lánitra* (this [land] beneath the sky) or *Ny anívon' ny ríaka* (this [all] in the centre of the sea). The Arabs seem to have known of Madagascar for a long time and probably traded with its people over many centuries.

Several words in the Malagasy language are of Arab origin. The old Malagasy calendar and the whole system of divination, or the defining of lucky and unlucky days, which is derived from that calendar, is also of Arabic origin. Traces of Arab influence are evident to this day, particularly in the north-west of the island.

Although the island of Madagascar is separated from the continent of Africa by nothing more than the narrow Mozambique Channel, it is not African and has few affinities with Africa. In fact, both as regards its plant and animal life, Madagascar exhibits many peculiarities. More than half the plants native to Madagascar are found there and nowhere else. Of the 220 species of birds in Madagascar about 100 are peculiar to the island. The large game animals which are so abundant in Africa are completely absent from the island. Madagascar's mammals are mostly small and harmless to man, with the possible exception of the wild pig, which has a relative in Africa. The country is noted for its lemurs, a small animal related to the monkey. There are a few lemurs in Africa, one of which is known as the bush baby, but one order of lemurs, of which there are more than a dozen varieties, is found only in Madagascar and its neighbouring islands. Madagascar also has several varieties of snakes, but none are venomous. The crocodile is found in swamps and rivers in the north and the east, and this animal is indeed dangerous, carrying off dogs and children when they go for water to the streams. For the botanist and natural history enthusiast Madagascar is a place of particular interest.

Geographically we may speak of Madagascar as the great African island, but the description does not fit its people. They are not African, but Malay/Polynesian in origin. Their language (for there is one language for the whole island) is related to Malay, Indonesian and some of the Polynesian languages. There is, however, an African element in their make-up, indicating some contacts with the African mainland in the course of their migration to Madagascar. The African influence in language, custom and even in physical appearance, is most marked among the Sakalava people of the west coast and the Bara in the south.[1]

Although a single people, with a common language, the

Malagasy differ widely from one another in physical characteristics and in their local dialects. The Mérina, in the central plateau, are distinguished by light colouring and straight hair, and it is among them that the relationship with the Malay and Indonesian peoples is most evident. Other tribes have darker colouring and curly or frizzy hair. There are fifteen or more separate tribes or peoples in the island, of whom the Mérina on the central plateau, the Sakaláva in the west, the Tsimihéty in the north and the Bétsimisáraka on the east coast, are the most numerous. The Betsiléo in the south are also a numerous people and they are very much akin to the Merina.

An important social class among the Merina is the Hova, and in fact early writers often spoke of the Merina people as the Hova. In time powerful Hova families gained an increasing ascendancy in the affairs of the central kingdom. The Merina may well have been the latest arrivals, ascending at once to the central plateau, which was named Imerina. They seem to have had from the beginning a capacity for organization superior to that of their neighbours. By the beginning of the nineteenth century the Merina kings had extended their control over a large part of the island, having first subdued the ruling chiefs by conquest. They liked to consider themselves rulers of all Madagascar.

In the Imerina plateau there were once several chiefs, each of whom ruled from his own capital or sacred city. These chiefs were related to one another, but the time was bound to come when one of them, or his successor, should aspire to control the whole of Imerina. The one who realized that ambition was Andría-nam-póin-imérina (king of the people of Imerina), and he reigned from 1787 to 1810. He consolidated his kingdom by alliance with neighbouring kings. He conquered many towns, one after the other, and then gave his attention to the largest of all, built on the highest hill, the town or city of An-tanán-arívo.

It took him three attempts to conquer this city on its 500-foot-high hill. He was not successful the first time as his army was decimated by smallpox, but eventually Antananarivo, or 'the city of a thousand' was in his power. It has remained as the capital of Madagascar to this day. Having

The 'Zoma' ('Friday'), the main city market in Antananarivo

subdued the whole of Imerina, which comprised the fertile central plateau of the island, Andrianampoinimerina turned his attention to the adjoining tribal areas. For he had declared, 'The whole of the island must belong to me; the sea must constitute the boundaries of my kingdom.' However, neither he nor those who followed him ever succeeded in this aim. It was not until Madagascar became a French possession in 1896 that the whole island came under one rule.

In the south was the rich country of the Betsiléo, and Andrianampoinimerina had no difficulty in overcoming the small independent territories, many of whose chiefs were at enmity with each other. The Bezánozáno in the east were advancing nearer to Antananarivo and were dealt with next. In the north-east the Sihánaka were repelled and fortifications established to keep them in check. The warlike Sakaláva in the west were harder to deal with, and there was considerable and extended conflict on the western border.

But it was as an administrator that the genius of Andrianampoinimerina was most clearly seen. He had gifts of organization far above the ordinary. He was concerned to promote the welfare and progress of his people. He made wise laws for their better government. He instituted a system of markets for the sale and barter of produce, and in order to facilitate trade he regulated a system of weights and measures. He had irrigation canals dug which drained much of the swampland round Antananarivo, and so increased considerably the rice-growing potential of the region. The wisdom of this ruler came from himself alone. He was under no foreign influence and, like all his subjects, was unable to read and write. He enacted penal legislation, which, though severe, was not repressive. Robbers were severely punished, but those caught stealing produce from a garden because of hunger were not punished, for, 'Whoever is hungry has a right to eat.'

Andrianampoinimerina was succeeded in 1810 by his son Radáma, who had been chosen and designated by him as his successor. Radama made contact with Europeans, both British and French, and gained a great deal from the contact. The British were anxious to see the suppression of the traffic in slaves. Each year many hundreds of Malagasy –

criminals, prisoners of war and other 'undesirable persons' – were sold as slaves. They were transported to Mauritius and then shipped elsewhere across the world. At the height of the trade some 3000–4000 people were shipped annually to Mauritius, Reunion and even to the Americas. The trade brought considerable wealth to Radama and to many of his nobles.[2] The agent of the Governor of Mauritius was an Irishman by the name of James Hastie, and it was his task to conclude a treaty with Radama for the cessation of this traffic in human lives. By way of compensation Radama was promised and provided with arms and ammunition and his army was trained by English military men. Radama was far-seeing enough to realize that the continuation of the slave trade would only decimate the country and impoverish his kingdom. He was therefore willing to bring the trade to an end so long as he was adequately compensated by the English.

Radama's soldiers received no pay, so the progress of his army, as it sought to carry out his orders to subdue the whole island to Merina rule, was a trail of pillage, slaughter and destruction. The army lived off the country, perpetrated needless destruction and inflicted great cruelty on all the inhabitants. When Captain le Sage visited Antananarivo in 1816 Radama's army amounted to probably 20,000 fighting men. These consisted of the ordinary peasants of the country, led by their local chieftains, under the supreme command of the king.

There were two sides to the Malagasy people as viewed by outsiders. On the one hand, they grasped eagerly the benefits of European civilization. They had, at least as regards the people of Imerina, an efficient organization of civil and military life, and they had a mind open to new ideas. But at the same time there was evidence of gross superstition and great cruelty. Many of their laws were harsh and the punishments meted out to wrongdoers were cruel and barbaric. Many of the coastal people, with whom the Europeans came into most frequent contact, lived in a most primitive fashion. They had gained a reputation for deceit and treachery. To be fair, one wonders how they might have earned any other kind of reputation, as most Europeans who visited their shores themselves tended to exploit and deceive the coastal peoples.

Madagascar as it was

The Malagasy are a religious people. They use with great frequency the name of God, who is known as Andríamánitra, meaning 'fresh, or enduring Prince'. The also use a term for God which designates him as Creator of all. But the potent force among them was embodied in the idols. Almost every household had its idols, which were usually kept in the ancestral or north-east corner of the house. No virtue or goodness was ascribed to the idols, only a supernatural power, which the people coveted and yet feared. The national idols were of recent origin as the kings in Imerina sought to extend their authority by ascribing great power to these national symbols.

One of the most pervasive aspects of Malagasy life is embodied in the idea of taboo, or *fady*, as the Malagasy term is. That which is *fady* may not be done or said or practised or, in the case of foods, may not be eaten. The various *fady* are handed down from the ancestors, and much of the resistance to change is due to the hold ancestral customs have over the people, including the *fady* handed down from previous generations. Some matters are *fady* over a wide area, while others apply to only one tribe, or even to a particular family. Unpopular *fady* can be circumvented, as was done by Ralambo, an early chief in Imerina. Beef was considered unhealthy and was therefore *fady*. But Ralambo changed the name of cattle from *jamoka* to the Bantu *omby* and was thus able to get his people to eat beef.

The most powerful influence over the people is that of divination, or *sikidy*. It was by *sikidy* that the destiny of a new-born child was determined, thus deciding whether it should be allowed to live or be destroyed. The new-born child deemed to have been born on an unlucky day was sometimes left at the entrance of the cattle-pen and exposed to the hooves of the cattle as they were driven home at night. If the cattle did not trample on the child then it was said to have been freed from its bad luck and it was allowed to live. The diviners used *sikidy* to determine the lucky day to begin a piece of work, or begin a journey, or get married.

The inhabitants of Madagascar seem to have been held in very low regard by Europeans. When Jones and Bevan were on their way to Madagascar in 1818 their boat called at the island of Reunion. General Lafitte, the governor of the island, enquired about their journey and their intentions. When he heard they were going to Madagascar to bring the gospel to its people he said to them, 'Why don't you begin by preaching to my dog? The Malagasy no more possess a spirit to respond to your message than has my dog.' Another well-wisher told them they would do better by preaching to the monkeys in the forest.

These were the people to whom David Jones went with the gospel message. Would he find them a people impossible to change and impervious to the gospel because of their superstitions and degraded ways? Was the message of Christ to prove powerless before such a people? Every true child of God believes the gospel to be the power of God for the salvation of everyone who believes. In Madagascar, through the labours of David Jones and his co-workers, the great power of the gospel was to be exhibited to a most remarkable degree.

Female slaves filling bamboos with water at the well

3.
David Jones begins his work

In 1820, David Jones, now restored to health and strength, was ready to return to Madagascar. But a storm had blown up over the question of the export of slaves from Madagascar. The British Government had sought to bring about the end of the traffic, and to that end had passed the Slave-Trade Abolition Act. To Governor Farquhar was given the unenviable task of implementing this act, which was not popular with the planters in Mauritius. Farquhar sent his agent, James Hastie, to Madagascar to conclude a treaty with King Radama for the cessation of the trade. The treaty provided that the traffic in slaves should cease and that Radama should be suitably compensated. Radama was to receive every year 1000 dollars each in gold and silver, a quantity of gunpowder and English muskets, together with English military uniforms for himself and for some of his officers. Because of ill-health Governor Farquhar had to return to England in 1818. There being insufficient time to consult with his superiors in London, he had to leave General Gage John Hall in charge as acting-governor. Hastie was to see to the implementation of the treaty and was to proceed to Antananarivo for that purpose. He arrived there in time to quell an outbreak of smallpox which had already claimed many lives. By introducing vaccination he was able to prevent further loss of life.

In the meantime there was trouble over the treaty. General Hall was refusing to pay the compensation without confirmatory orders from London. He recalled Hastie from Antananarivo. It appears that slaves were still entering Mauritius, and Acting-Governor Hall doubted the sincerity of the efforts being made to suppress the trade. He declared that the treaty was 'trash and nonsense' and went on to say, in answer to Hastie's remonstrance, 'Much we care for British faith among a parcel of savages.' General Hall's methods were too blunt and forthright for the situation. He considered Governor Farquhar's cautious policy to be devious and ineffective. Hall was no diplomat and, though he was not averse to stopping the trade, his outspoken manner and rigorous methods undid much of Farquhar's work and brought about his own recall from Mauritius in 1818. Mervyn Brown says of him, 'It is impossible to question Hall's sincerity, [but] he stands convicted of the charge of stupidity. He completely failed to understand Farquhar's overall strategy ... The effect of his action was to destroy Britain's credibility with Radama and to postpone for several years the measure which was to be the most effective weapon against the slave trade in the region.'[1]

Radama was naturally very incensed at this change of attitude, and felt himself put to shame before his people for trusting the foreigners. The breaking of the treaty gave the English a bad name among all the people, and it became a saying among them that if a person broke an agreement, and in particular if he showed some cleverness in getting out of his side of the bargain, he was 'deceitful as the

David Jones begins his work

English'. Radama threatened to revive the whole slave trade if the agreement was not honoured and the promised compensation paid by the British.

Governor, now Sir Robert, Farquhar, returned to Mauritius in July 1820. He lost no time in sending James Hastie back to Madagascar to try to retrieve the situation. David Jones had the opportunity of accompanying him, not just to Toamasina, but to Antananarivo, the centre of the Hova kingdom. He went with the blessing and goodwill of Governor Farquhar, who had already petitioned the London Missionary Society to begin a work in Madagascar. James Hastie too was in sympathy with the aims of the mission. Two years earlier, when David Jones was at Toamasina, Radama had invited him to come up to the plateau. But, on the other hand, there was the anger and confusion caused by the breaking of the treaty. David Jones may well have pondered as to the wisdom of proceeding to Madagascar at such a time.

On their arrival at Toamasina they learned that Radama had forbidden any Englishman to visit Antananarivo. Hastie, however, was not deterred and sent a message to the king, declaring his intention to travel to the capital and asking for permission for David Jones to accompany him. Permission was granted and Radama received Hastie joyfully. His delight at seeing his friend again overrode his disgust at the perfidious actions of the English. But the treaty was not renewed without a great deal of anguished discussion and parley. As had been already agreed, the British Government was to supply Radama with quantities of guns and ammunition. Now Hastie agreed that his soldiers should be taught military drill and he also undertook, on his own authority, to send some young men to England for training. It was ultimately agreed, as part of the settlement of the revived treaty, that ten young men should be sent to Mauritius and ten to England to be educated. Radama saw too that the arrival of the English missionary could be of benefit to his people. But he made it plain that he only accepted the Christian religion so long as the greater number of missionaries were artisans, able to 'make his people good workmen as well as good Christians'.

In writing to the L.M.S. in London confirming Radama's acceptance of the mission, David Jones had this to say concerning the young Malagasy ruler: 'The King is a young man about 29 years old who has subjected almost all Madagascar to himself and united the chieftains and made them submissive to him so that an end is almost put to all wars between the petty chiefs in Madagascar. He is very powerful and can in a few days raise an army of 100,000 men. He has already 2,000 who can go through their exercises by English commands ... It is astonishing what government he has over his people – they tremble before him and yet he is always very merry and affable with them.'[2]

The supply of arms and ammunition meant further wars and more slaughter of outlying tribes by Radama's soldiers, so the suppression of the slave trade, beneficial though it was, resulted in much suffering for many people. Radama's expeditions to the coast and to other areas outside Imerina resulted in devastation and destruction on a large scale. Even those who surrendered to Radama's lieutenants were likely to be cruelly murdered, their cattle and goods seized and their villages burned to the ground. These were some of the actions of the king who shrewdly sought education and enlightenment for his people. The barbaric and the semi-civilized dwelt side by side in Radama and his subjects.

David Jones was constrained to wait until Hastie had concluded his negotiations with Radama. He began his work in earnest on 8 December 1820, surely a red-letter day in the history of the great island! He began with three pupils, two of whom were nephews of Radama. In the absence of proper writing materials they wrote with pointed sticks on pieces of board which had been greased and sprinkled with ashes. The number of pupils soon increased to forty, and the king had a special building erected, of which he himself laid the foundation. Still the number of pupils grew and before long they could be numbered in hundreds. Certainly there were those who thought their children were being taught only to make them more valuable slaves. But it seemed that the majority welcomed the opportunity to learn, and soon many began to show an interest in the New Testament.

David Griffiths arrived in May 1821. He had been a fellow student of David Jones at Neuaddlywyd. They were firm friends and worked together for many years. Others soon joined them, including another David Jones, who was also a former pupil of Dr Thomas Phillips. He became known as David Johns, to distinguish him from his namesake. The Malagasy, not being able to distinguish in their speech between 'Jones' and 'Johns', called David Jones *Jonjy Lava* (tall Jones) and David Johns *Jonjy Fohy* (short Jones). James Cameron was a Scot and was by trade a carpenter. He had read widely and had a knowledge of many subjects and he became a tower of strength to the growing mission.

Young and old were all eager to learn, so a school was opened in the grounds of the palace for the officers of the army and their wives, and it soon had three hundred learners. Early in 1824 several of the more advanced students were sent, with the consent of the king, to open schools and begin teaching in the surrounding villages.

In 1826 the long-awaited printing-press arrived. After an initial set-back caused by the death of the printer, it was now possible to print primers and reading material for the schoolchildren, as well as passages of Scripture which had been translated. There was now real progress. By 1828 the one small school with three pupils had grown to thirty-two schools where 4000 children and young people were learning to read and receiving Christian instruction. Literacy was increasing among the general population too, so that many who had never entered a school were able to read and were eager for books.

Up to this point no one, so far as was known, had responded to the message, nor had any been baptized. Nevertheless there was a keen interest on the part of many. Then the king gave his approval that any who wished to be baptized were free to do so. The missionaries opened preaching places and began by explaining the catechism and delivering courses of lectures to the more advanced students. They then began preaching, first in the school-houses, then in a building erected as a place of worship. All were invited to attend the preaching, adults as well as children, but at first very few accepted the invitation. The people were still wholly given to idolatry and to a chronic moral laxity. The stern requirements of the Christian ethic were more than they were prepared to accept.

Nevertheless in ten short years a vast amount had been accomplished. Portions of Scripture had been translated and were in use, and many thousands of children and adults had

Women washing clothes in the River Ikopa

learned to read. Schools were being opened in the surrounding villages. The government still viewed the work of the mission with favour and were pleased with the skills in carpentry, building, brickmaking and similar trades which were being imparted to eager young men by the artisan missionaries. Yet the missionaries realized that the true object of their work was not so far attained: no Malagasy had as yet professed faith in Jesus Christ. There was much interest, but no commitment of heart and mind to the gospel. Radama the king was the chief encourager and supporter of the work of the mission. He suppressed the murmurs and complaints of those who would oppose the work. When the children who were being educated in the mission school began to speak disparagingly of the traditional idols and were reported to the king for so doing he bade the complainants mind their own business and let the children mind their lessons. But his support of the mission was qualified by his personal indifference to the message brought by the missionaries. He encouraged the children in their lessons and rewarded the most successful, but was himself unmoved by the gospel.

The Malagasy children were apt and diligent pupils. The missionaries were constantly amazed at the progress they made. We can picture a class of children, clean and neatly dressed, both boys and girls, and attending with diligence and enthusiasm to their lessons. The children were taught hymns, translated or composed by the missionaries, and because of their fondness for music they sang hymns at home and along the streets as well as at school. The king visited the schools from time to time and encouraged the children in their lessons. He was pleased at the arrival of the printing-press and directed that six young men should be apprenticed to the printing trade.

This favourable climate was soon to change. Radama was only thirty-six years of age, but his constitution had been weakened by the rigours of camp life, irregular habits and intemperate indulgences. On 27 June 1828 the king died. There is no doubt that he was raised up by God at a crucial time in the history of the Malagasy people. He had opened for his nation contact with the outside world, he had concluded with England a treaty which brought an end to the destructive slave trade and closed one of the great slave markets of the world. Above all, he had opened his country and exposed his people to the gospel message. Though he himself never responded to that message he weakened the power of superstition by exposing the craftiness of the priests and the jugglery of the diviners, and by abolishing infanticide he saved the lives of multitudes of new-born infants. Madagascar, through his enlightened policy, was just coming out of the darkness of paganism and superstition to a new era of enlightenment. But on the death of Radama the country was to reverse that direction and return to darkness and fear.

Street in Toamasina

4.
A new queen

The news of the death of King Radama was kept hidden from the people for some days. The band played as usual in the palace courtyard every afternoon, and the king was reported to be improving in health. The delay was fatal to the aims of his friends and to his lawful successor. The king had nominated Prince Rakótobé, eldest son of his own sister, to be his successor. But there was a reactionary party which was determined to undo the work of Radama and to reverse his liberal policy. The leader of this party was Ránaválona, one of his wives. She was determined to be queen. Being secretly advised of the death of the king she acted quickly and decisively. She promised great rewards and high honours to two of her partisans if they would place her on the throne.

The two officers won over some of the priests and judges and collected the troops in the capital under their command. Two days later a *kabáry*, or public proclamation, was made for administering the oath of allegiance to the one appointed by the king to be his successor. At that *kabary* Ranavalona was named as the lawful queen. In the meantime Prince Rakotobe, who was only seventeen years of age, was seized at night, carried away to a distant place and beside a newly-dug grave was speared to death and there buried. He was the first pupil in the class of 1820 and a friend of the missionaries. There is every reason to believe he had embraced the gospel to the saving of his soul.

There were political reactions to this seizure of power by Ranavalona, both within the country and in relations with the European powers of Britain and France. Our main concern in this history is Ranavalona's treatment of the Christians, but her character, and that of her reign, reflected bitterly on all her subjects, and led to the rupture of the friendly relations which had been building up between Madagascar and certain of the European powers. Compared with King Radama, whom she succeeded by bloodshed and violence, Ranavalona was reactionary and retrograde in every way. She seemed determined to lead the nation back into the darkness and cruelty and slavish dependence on the idols from which it, or portions of it, were just emerging.

One writer has said this about her: 'The days of this queen present a lurid picture. Out of a background of darkness and blood rises the figure of a terrible woman – dressed in Paris fashion, yet the devotee of idols; a sovereign possessed by the lust of power and of cruelty; a ruler living in seclusion, because too divine to be approached by her people, who had to carry out her will at the threat of horrors of torture; a queen whose deliberate aim was the extermination of the manhood of all other than the Hova tribe, as a means of preventing revolt and for the enrichment of her favourites and soldiers by female slaves and possessions. Yet this ruthless woman was a doting mother, whose only son, strong in the consciousness of that love, dared with impunity to counteract, where possible, her nefarious decrees of slaughter.'[1]

A new queen

The missionaries Freeman and Johns, who were serving in Madagascar at this time, say that the queen was not a woman of superior intelligence, but she was of great determination of mind. She was only slightly acquainted with reading and writing. Her soul was completely bound to the superstitions of the country and she deeply venerated the national idols. It was the idols, she declared, who had put her on the throne. No doubt she genuinely believed that to depart from the idols would bring calamity on the Hova nation. Be that as it may, she had a mind which was not open to new ideas, a heart which was full of cruelty and a disposition to stubbornness which boded ill for all who crossed her will.

Almost all of the late king's family were put to death, either by spear or by lingering starvation. Then when her position was secure the coronation ceremony was held, in which the royal idols had a prominent place. During the mourning for the late king all school work was forbidden as well as much general work in the country. Nevertheless the new queen said she had no intention of changing anything that Radama had begun. At the beginning she seemed uncertain as to which course to adopt towards the Christians. She vacillated a great deal, forbidding one day what she permitted the next. This made it possible for the work to go ahead, but only in an atmosphere of fearfulness and uncertainty. For the six months that the schools were closed the missionaries pressed on with the work of translation and printing. The new printer, Edward Baker, having arrived, the press was able to be worked at full speed. Gospels were produced in thousands as well as lesson books for the schools.

How to gain enough time to complete the printing and binding of the Scriptures was what now occupied the minds of the missionaries. For it was evident that the liberal policy of Radama was gone and that opposition to their work was growing. Though the queen was uncertain what to do about the Christians, it was clear that a change for the worse was imminent. But one essential task, the completion of the Malagasy Bible, was still far from being achieved.

The queen sent officers to the missionaries to thank them for what they had done for the country and to ask them what else they proposed to teach the people. Otherwise they would be asked to depart. Their proposal to revive the teaching of Greek and Hebrew to the senior pupils did not appeal to the queen. Could they not teach the manufacture of soap or gunpowder? The missionaries were not prepared to assist in the manufacture of gunpowder, but the ever-resourceful James Cameron was prepared to try his hand at soap-making. 'Give us a week,' he said, 'and we'll bring an answer to the queen.'

The problem was to make soap from materials available on the spot, for the manufacture of soap from imported raw materials would not satisfy the queen's wishes. James Cameron applied his knowledge of chemistry and searched through books of reference. He tried various fats and oils and the ashes of different kinds of wood. When the officers returned he was able to show them two small bars of tolerably good soap. The queen was delighted and at once made an agreement with him to commence the large-scale manufacture of soap and to teach the same to her people. We read that in 1830, when there was a distribution of 425 newly-printed New Testaments, the distribution included '20 copies to Mr Cameron for those recently appointed by the Government to learn soap-making'.[2] In his L.M.S. handbook, *The Madagascar Mission*,[3] the Rev. James Sibree comments that 'It may be said with perfect truth that it was largely to the production of these two little bars of soap that the missionaries were allowed to continue their work for several years longer, and to lay deep and firm the foundations of the Malagasy Church.'

In December 1828 the schools were allowed to open again, but not all of them. Then almost at once some 700 teachers and senior pupils were drafted into the army. This put fear into the hearts of many parents and as a result school enrolments dropped by half. Encouraged by the example of the queen, many of the population gave themselves with increasing zeal to idol worship and to all its attendant superstitions.

On the other hand, there was clear evidence that God was working in many hearts. The two places of worship, at Ambódin' Ando-hálo and Ambáto-na-kánga, proved too small and crowds of 2,000 and even 3,000 gathered to worship each Sunday, some having to stand outside at the doors and windows. There was a deep earnestness on the part of the worshippers and a desire to understand and to receive the saving truths of the gospel. People sought out the missionaries in their homes in order to enquire further about the gospel.

On 29 May 1831 twenty people were baptized at Ambodin' Andohalo, and on the following Sunday a further eight were baptized at Ambatonakanga. Both of these places are in the city of Antananarivo. Thus the first-fruits of the gospel were being gathered in. How the hearts of the missionaries must have rejoiced, but how much greater the rejoicing in heaven! These new converts met together around the Lord's Table, and soon afterwards, on 12 June, the first Malagasy congregation covenanted together as a church. They were few in number and young in the faith and they already had some inkling of what might befall them. But their Lord and Saviour was Jesus Christ, and he had promised that the gates of Hades should not prevail against his church, of which they were a part. Very soon they were going to need that assurance, and in their need of it they were to prove the truth of it.

Of this first company of new believers two were man and wife. Raíni-tsi-héva, the husband, had gained much wealth and influence by the practice of divination. He was much sought after to use his powers in the choosing of lucky days and in similar activities. At his conversion he destroyed the instruments of his divination, except for two, which he handed to the missionaries. He publicly declared his faith in Christ, was baptized and then took his place with the schoolchildren in order to learn to read the Gospels. At his baptism he took the name of Paul, for he said he too was the chief of sinners. On account of his former way of life he became known as Paul the Diviner.

The years from 1832 to 1834 were a period of great uncertainty and fearfulness. On the one hand the missionaries continued their work without interruption, particularly that which had to do with the printing-press. But a message was sent to David Griffiths to tell him his ten years were up. This was in terms of an old law which said that Europeans could only stay in the country for ten years unless they became Malagasy subjects. He was given five months to pack his baggage and then was given an extension of time. He obtained permission to remain a year longer and then his stay was extended indefinitely. He seems finally to have left in 1835. But two other missionaries were abruptly ordered to leave, even though one of them, the Rev. Theophilus Atkinson, had not been in the country a year.

A message came from the queen forbidding any who were in the army to be baptized or to partake of Holy Communion. Then the pupils in the schools were forbidden to attend Communion. An earlier order had forbidden slaves to learn to read and write, but many had, of course, already attended school. This order was intended to keep the slave population in their inferior state. By the end of 1831 there was a general prohibition: no member of the Malagasy community could be baptized or partake of Holy Communion. Nevertheless the desire to be numbered among the Christians was still strong, and there were some who came secretly to the homes of the missionaries and there they were baptized and gathered with their teachers around the Table of the Lord.

In spite of all these harassments the preaching of the gospel continued. The chapels were open each Sunday and full of worshipping people. Generally one or other of the missionaries preached the Word. There were also other meetings for worship and instruction almost every day throughout the week. These were held in different parts of the city and were all led by the people themselves. The speakers were Malagasy Christians. All their meetings included the singing of hymns. The Malagasy people are fond of music and when Christian hymns were introduced they took to them with great enthusiasm. Some hymns were translated from English and others were composed by missionaries or by Malagasy Christians. A small hymn-book was produced and was put to good use from the start. So by singing, praying, preaching and the reading of Scripture the word of the gospel spread and at the same time sank deeply into the hearts of many of the people. No wonder David Johns declared, 'I believe this church will prevail as long as the world lasts.'

One very interesting incident belongs to this time. A married couple had applied to a maker of idols to have a household god made for them to hang up in their house. On the appointed day they went to collect the idol and found it was not ready. They were obliged to wait until the evening. The man had been to the forest and brought home the branch of a tree, from which he began to prepare the idol. The visitors had a meal with him while the idol was being finished. The idol-maker gathered up the chips and broken pieces of wood and pushed them under the pot of boiling rice. Afterwards they paid for their idol and returned home.

Soon afterwards this couple were visited by a young Christian, who had his Bible with him. He read to them from the Scriptures, and it so happened that he read from Isaiah chapter 44, including the verses:

> 'Half of the wood he burns in the fire;
>   over it he prepares his meal,
>   he roasts his meat and eats his fill. . .
> From the rest he makes a god, his idol.'

The woman was astonished at the exact description of what she had just witnessed. She was convinced of the truth of the gospel, abandoned her idols and became a true disciple of the Lord. We shall meet her again in the course of this history.

Several events occurred about this time which seem to have particularly incensed the queen and to have aroused the jealousy of many government officials. These men thought that if proceedings were taken against the Christians and their property confiscated they could enrich themselves by sharing in the spoils. One of the most inveterate enemies of the gospel was an official of the palace, Ratsímanísa by name. If the queen faltered in her resolve he was only too ready to urge her on.

The first incident caused a great stir. It came about through the activities of Raini-tsí-an-dávaka, a keeper of a government idol in a village to the north of the capital. He had acquired property and, being an industrious person, he was comfortably well off. But during 1832 he suffered various calamities. First his wife and soon afterwards his child died. Some of his slaves ran away and others died. These things preyed on his mind. About this time he had occasion to go to the village of Paul the Diviner, and there he heard the gospel from the lips of Paul himself. As a result he appeared to have responded to the message and in company with Paul he visited one of the missionaries. He began immediately to talk to relations and neighbours about the resurrection and the last judgement. He was urged to desist and to study the Scriptures more closely before beginning to preach. But the advice annoyed him and he kept on. He claimed that God was teaching him independently of the Bible. In spite of remonstrances from the Christians he continued proclaiming his half-baked notions, which tended to combine respect for the idols with some of the tenets of Christianity. He always claimed, however, that what he taught and the message of the missionaries were substantially the same. His personal life was without blame. In the course of two years he had gathered about two hundred followers.

In 1834 Rainitsiandavaka sent word to the queen intimating that he had an important message for her. The jealousy of the government was aroused and he and his followers were summoned to the palace. This delighted them as they felt sure they could bring the queen round to their way of thinking. She sent a messenger to them on the road and adjured them that if their message were not true they should return home at once, but if it were true they were to come forward and deliver it. They came to the palace and were closely questioned by the judges and officers concerning their beliefs. 'God has told us these things,' they said, 'and God cannot lie.' They were questioned over two or three days, and one question concerned their statement that all mankind was descended from the same parents. 'Do you mean to affirm that we Hova and the Mozambiques are from the same parents?' they were asked. They replied that it was so. This grossly offended the vanity of the Hova, for they despised the Mozambiques, who had been brought over from East Africa and were employed by many of the Hova as slaves. It was this assertion that helped to seal the doom of Rainitsiandavaka and his followers. He and three of his principal followers were put to death at

A new queen

once. They were placed, head down, in a rice pit, and boiling water was poured on them. Seventeen of their followers were compelled to take the *tangéna* ordeal, under which eight died. The rest were sold into slavery and their property confiscated, adding to the wealth of some of the queen's officers. The sect was crushed, but the incident helped to bring further suspicion on the Christians.

As the year 1834 drew to a close there was increasing evidence of a work of God in the hearts of many of the people. Nearly 200 had applied for admission to the fellowship of the church. This request could only be granted in secrecy. Bible classes were formed for the study of the Scriptures and it became clear that the hearts and consciences of many were awakened, not only in the capital, but also in the surrounding villages.

The Malagasy have a system of unlucky days, that is, on certain days of the week it is forbidden by order of the idols to work in the rice fields. The Christians were unwilling to respect these *fady*, or prohibitions, on the premise that an idol is nothing and can safely be ignored. A young Christian was forced to desist from working in his rice field on a prohibited day and, supposedly on the order of the idol, was sentenced to be cut in pieces lest the crops be destroyed. These matters were reported to the queen, who ordered the young man to submit to the *tangéna* ordeal. He was declared innocent, to the great joy of the Christians. A few days later he was brought into the city in a *filanjána*, or carrying chair, accompanied by a large number of Christians wearing white *lamba*, or shawls, and singing hymns of praise. The queen saw the procession from a distance and was not at all pleased to hear it was a procession of Christians rejoicing that one of their number had been declared innocent by the *tangena*, an ordeal she had ordered.

It may be as well to explain at this point what is involved in the *tangena* ordeal. It would be difficult to ascertain, or even guess, how many Malagasy, innocent of any crime, have perished under this fearful ordeal. Mervyn Brown estimates that many thousands perished in this way during the reign of Ranavalona. In their *Narrative of the Persecutions of the Christians in Madagascar* J.J. Freeman and David Johns describe the *tangena* ordeal: 'To be pronounced innocent by the ordeal removes a man above suspicion, however clear may be the proof of his guilt; to be condemned by it is a demonstration of guilt, however strong the proof of his innocence on other grounds. The ordeal consists in administering an emetic draught, formed of the nut of the tangena (*Tenghinia venenifera Madagascariensis*), accompanied with a portion of the juice of the banana tree. This draught acts on a stomach previously supplied with a large meal of boiled rice; after eating which, three pieces of the skin of a fowl, killed for the occasion, are swallowed. If the three pieces are returned from the stomach, innocence is demonstrated, and the party is pronounced *Velona* (living), and is in due time led by his friends to his village with much pomp and ceremony.'[4]

In another place they describe how two of the Christians had the *tangena* administered to them. The administrator pronounces curses over the head of the victim, and then he is given copious draughts of warm water to induce vomiting. If a brief form of cursing is pronounced over the victim he is able to drink the warm water soon and vomit out the poison, but if the form of cursing is prolonged the victim may become very ill and death may result. In the example quoted by the missionaries, the cursing was very brief over one of the two Christians, and he was speedily delivered. But a long time was occupied in denouncing the curses on the other and even though he drank five or six gallons of water his strength began to fail and excruciating pains came over him. His health was much affected and his sight was impaired. Thus those who administer the *tangena* can to some extent anticipate the result by the length of time which elapses before the victim is allowed to drink the warm water. There is no semblance of justice in this cruel ordeal, which was outlawed by the succeeding ruler of the Hova.

Spies were sent out by the queen to inform on the Christians. Garbled reports were brought back from their meetings, including the notion that Jehovah was the first king of the English and Jesus Christ was the second. One informer came to the palace weeping for effect and asking for a spear to destroy himself lest he should see the calamities which were about to come upon his country. He said the Christians were despising divination and the idols, and that they held assemblies at night which were carried on and addressed by slaves. The queen was exceedingly incensed at these reports and it is said she burst into tears of grief and rage and swore she would put a stop to these proceedings. She gave orders to summon all the people, even young children, to a great *kabary*, or assembly, to be held at the capital on Sunday, 1 March 1835. In the meantime an order was given to make a list of the houses in which prayer meetings were held, as well as the names of all who had been baptized. The queen was astonished at the numbers and expressed her feelings against the Christians with great violence.

There was, however, still much uncertainty as to the course to be adopted towards the Christians. The enmity of the queen herself was only too evident. Some of her advisers were also avowed enemies of Christianity and were determined to bring about the downfall of the Christians. But when the queen asked her officers for their views on the matter one of them was bold enough to testify that the Christians had proved themselves to be upright, diligent, faithful and trustworthy: 'If I tell them to go anywhere on business, whether by day or night, they go; whatever I desire them to do, they do it, and scarcely ever have I cause to be angry with any of them. Besides this, they certainly possess more intelligence and knowledge than most others in the country. Your predecessors, Madam, put a great value on wise, faithful and intelligent subjects.' So spoke Rainingitabé, one of the queen's advisers. Another officer spoke of the useful arts which had been introduced by the Europeans, and of the reproach which would fall on the country if any of those who had learned those arts should be put to death.

But it was too late for these final pleas on behalf of the Christians to have any effect. The queen was obsessed with the idea that the Christians were interfering with her sovereignty and were belittling the idols, and for that they must suffer. On the previous Sunday to the discussion with her officers, the queen had returned to the palace in the late evening and in passing the chapel at Ambatonakanga she had heard the singing of hymns. She had observed to those with her, 'These people will not leave off until some of them lose their heads.'

One of the judges had a daughter whose habit it was to worship with the Christians. On the Sunday following, 22 February, he solemnly warned his daughter not to go to Ambatonakanga to worship. However, she went all the same. When he returned to his house and found she was not there, he proceeded at once to the chapel. He was amazed to see such a large congregation, but he did not find his daughter. Returning home he said to some of his servants, 'You will never see such a congregation again, for the queen does not approve.' This remark greatly increased the fears and suspicions of the Christians, for this man was well placed to know the queen's mind.

On the following Thursday the usual public service was held at Ambatonakanga, and one of the Malagasy leaders was requested to conduct the meeting and deliver the address. He preached an impressive message from the text, 'Lord, save us: we perish' (Matt. 8:25, AV). It was the last public service of worship to be held in that building.

On the same afternoon the missionaries were commanded to assemble and to hear a message from the queen. The officers came to the appointed place, led by Ratsimanisa, the strongest opponent of the Christian gospel. The gist of the queen's message was: 'That which has been established by my ancestors I cannot permit to be changed: I am neither ashamed nor afraid to maintain the customs of my ancestors. And with regard to religious worship, whether on Sunday or not, the practice of baptism and the existence of a society [that is, membership of a church] – these things cannot be done by my subjects in my country. But if there be knowledge of the arts and sciences which will be beneficial to my subjects in the country, teach that, for it is good.'

The missionaries replied to this, saying they had left their native country to teach the good Word of God, that this Word is beneficial to those who obey it and that it renders illustrious and prosperous those kingdoms which receive it. They earnestly entreated the queen not to suppress this teaching, but to allow them to teach it, together with the arts and sciences. To this the queen sent an evasive reply, but the time for diplomatic exchange of correspondence was over. Events were now moving to a climax.

Female slaves filling bamboos with water at the well

5.
The blow falls

Sunday, 1 March 1835 was the occasion of the fateful *kabary* or public proclamation called by the queen. The dawning of the day was greeted by the firing of cannon, intended to strike awe into the hearts of the people. For days past fear and superstition had ruled, rumours had flown thick and fast, and the normally loquacious Malagasy were silent. There was no conversation, just a simple greeting as they met. All were afraid lest anything they said should be heard by spies and reported to the government. Almost every family had some relative who prayed and whose name was known to the government.

Now the day had arrived, and all in the city and in the

surrounding villages, 'even to a child a cubit high', began to assemble as ordered in the vast I-máha-másina plain on the west side of the city of Antananarivo. The soldiers were drawn up on parade, the cannon continued to thunder, and the people assembled in the place appointed for each village and for each quarter of the city. It was estimated that 100,000 people were gathered to hear the queen's proclamation. The queen's message declared first her confidence in the idols and her determination to continue the customs of her ancestors. She would treat as criminals all who refused to do homage to the idols or who despised divination: 'As to baptisms, societies, places of worship and the sabbath, who rules in this land? "Is it not I who rule?" says Ranavalomanjaka. These things are not our ancestral customs, therefore they are unlawful.'

Those who had simply attended school as pupils were not condemned even if they had worshipped there, but all those who had been baptized or who had opened their houses for prayer, whether pupils or soldiers or slaves, were given one month to confess and to come forward and accuse themselves, 'But if any come first and accuse you, I denounce death against you, says Ranavalomanjaka.' The queen also found fault with the Christians because they would no longer swear by all that is sacred in heaven and earth, nor by the twelve sovereigns, nor by the sacred idols, but they changed the customs of the ancestors and would simply reply, 'True', when questioned. 'And when you are asked, "Do you swear it?" you reply, "True". I wonder at this! What indeed is that word "True"?' The believers had quickly learned the injunction of their Lord: 'Do not swear at all . . . Simply let your "Yes" be "Yes", and your "No," "No".'

Two provincial officers then came forward and declared on behalf of all the people that the things of which the queen disapproved had been done in ignorance and not in disobedience. They reminded the queen that Radama had welcomed the Europeans when they came and that he had exhorted the schoolchildren to learn all they could from the white men, and that much good had come to the kingdom as a result. However, they confessed their guilt and craved the queen's pardon and asked her to accept a bullock and a dollar as a fine for having displeased her.

Next day a message was returned from the palace saying that the queen did not consent to receiving the proferred fine. She said, among other things, 'You could not wait even one month, you could not return home at all. As you appear anxious on account of your crimes, I will give you a week to accuse yourselves and not a whole month. The soldiers are to confess to the principal officers, the people are to confess to the judges, and the scholars to those who rule over them. And remember that next Sunday is the last day; unless you send in your names by that day you die wilfully.'

During the next few days many people, including the twelve principal school teachers, were in a hurry to come forward in self-accusation and with much servility begged the queen's pardon. These included some who had worshipped as Christian believers. Now, in the hour of trial, like Peter of old, they said, 'I don't know him.' Some said, 'I went to the meetings out of curiosity, but seeing the evil of it I ceased to go.' Others said, 'We went along with a lot of other people, but we didn't know what it was all about.' There were some too of whom the missionaries had expected better things who made similar excuses.

So Christianity was dead. The queen congratulated herself that the fear of death had driven faith out of every breast. A government official cited a hymn he had often heard the Christians singing before the suppression of Christianity. 'I have no fear of death, for Jesus is ever nigh,' they used to sing. He scoffed at their claim, declaring that they were singing a lie, for, he said, he had seen them coming almost out of breath to denounce themselves and so avoid death. He said he did not believe there was one real believer in the country apart from the Europeans. At the first threat of death all the believers had recanted.

But this was far from being the case. Certainly the church had been sifted and much chaff had been blown away by the wind of perscecution, but the majority of the believers stood firm. The very taunts of their enemies caused many to look again at the promises of God and to face squarely the consequences of remaining true to his Word. One Christian from a distant district came forward and said, 'Yes, he had prayed.' When asked how often, he said he could not tell, but for the past three or four years he had prayed to God several times a day. He witnessed a good confession before his accusers, who heard from his lips a clear and faithful presentation of the gospel.

The missionaries still remained in Antananarivo and were busy completing the revision and printing of the Old Testament. But they could be of very limited help to their Malagasy friends. No preaching services were allowed and those who visited the missionaries in their homes did so at dead of night and in peril of their lives. Already the Christians were learning to stay their souls on God and on his Word. A company of believers agreed to meet in the vestry of the church at Ambatonakanga. They were joined by a senior officer in the army, who deplored the injustice done to the Christians and who was moved to join their company. He proved a faithful follower of Christ and a great help to his fellow Christians. His wife too became a believer. These people afterwards testified to the strength and blessing they had experienced in these times of prayer.

During the same week three or four Christian women were together in the house of one of their number. Their husbands had gone to the city to give themselves up and as they sat in the house they were full of fears and forebodings. One of them gave voice to the thoughts of all, saying, 'I have often thought that if persecution should arise I would have no strength to bear it, and I fear all my religion is delusive.' To this downcast and dejected group a fellow Christian came late in the evening. He asked them the cause of their dejection and they told him of all the anxieties and fears of the day just past and of their fears for the future. He asked them if they had read the Word of God during the day. No, they had had no opportunity. Had they prayed to God? No, they had tried to pray, but had been overpowered by fear. He chided them for neglecting prayer and the reading of the Word. The Lord who is mighty had promised help in time of need. He then read to them Psalm 46, which begins, 'God is our refuge and strength, an ever-present help in trouble.' He commented briefly on it and then knelt down and prayed fervently that God would strengthen them and remove their fears. One of these women remarked long afterwards that they had hardly ever been afraid again. One of them was later sold into slavery on account of her faith.

The blow falls

On the morning of 9 March the queen's message was brought to the assembled people by the judges and officers. Christianity was to be proscribed totally and completely and those who had Christian books were to hand them over to be returned to the missionaries. The worship of the idols was to be maintained and if anyone changed his religion, the offender would be put to death. None were in fact put to death or sold into slavery at this time, but about 400 officers were reduced in rank and about 2000 others were fined. Some books were returned, but by no means all. Most of the Christians were determined to keep at least a Gospel or a hymn-book, though the fear of death ensured some compliance with the order. Orders to collect Christian books were sent even to distant outposts, for the Scriptures had been disseminated far and wide. However, although the queen's orders had been faithfully transmitted, her command was scarcely obeyed at all in provincial districts.

The work of the mission was now virtually at an end. Apart from some private counselling the missionaries had no contact with their people. They realized that the divine command to preach the gospel transcended any human edict, but to continue their work in the prevailing climate seemed to be not just difficult, but impossible. They had sent word to the directors of the mission in London advising them of the situation, but they knew that more than a year would elapse before they could receive a reply. So they were cast upon their own resources. The government had assumed that their design in coming to Madagascar was political, and to continue in the country when they had no possibility of contact with the Christians would lend credence to that view. There seemed nothing to do but to withdraw – not to abandon the work as a lost cause, but to wait for a more propitious time to recommence it.

Accordingly it was decided that most of the missionary band should withdraw at once. Freeman, Cameron, Chick and Kitching left for England in June 1835. Only David Johns and Edward Baker remained, for the task of translating and printing the Scriptures was still unfinished. In the Old Testament Ezekiel to Malachi and a portion of Job had not yet been printed. Edward Baker had to do all the work himself, as the Malagasy who had learned to work at the printing-press were no longer permitted to do so. During this time David Johns, in co-operation with one of the Christians, translated John Bunyan's *Pilgrim's Progress* into Malagasy. Six handwritten copies were made available to the Christians, while one copy was sent to England, where it was printed and copies were later sent out to the Christians in Madagascar. This Christian classic was of immense value to the believers and was prized by them, next to the Bible, as their most valuable treasure. In the Malagasy language the names of people (often appearing inordinately long to foreigners) are usually descriptive of some quality concerning birth, parentage or character, and thus the language lends itself most aptly to the translation of John Bunyan's masterpiece. *Pilgrim's Progess* is highly prized in Madagascar to this day.

So far as any action by the authorities was concerned, the next year or so remained fairly quiet. But it was 'a year of suspense, anxiety and pain to the missionary families that remained', as Edward Baker wrote. Although the government seemed unwilling to proceed against the missionaries themselves, their servants were subjected to the *tangena*, and the queen ordered that a newborn baby belonging to one of them should be suffocated because it was supposedly born on a 'day of bad omen'. Government oppression of the people became more and more cruel. Sunday was purposely desecrated by public amusements, while vice and poverty increased.

Meanwhile the Christians sought each other out and encouraged one another in the faith. There was need at all times for great caution, and they found a way of identifying one another by reciting Jeremiah 38:15, which says, 'If I give you an answer, will you not kill me?' The reply was in the following verse: 'As surely as the Lord lives, who has given us breath, I will neither kill you nor hand you over to those who are seeking your life.' The Christians were forbidden to sing, yet they longed to sing the songs of Zion. Some played the tunes on the native *valíha* (a type of guitar made from bamboo), while others followed the words in their minds. The number of believers continued to increase and at the same time they grew in spiritual knowledge and strength. The Lord's Supper was occasionally administered and some even received baptism. Companies of Christians used to meet in remote places where they could pray and sing in safety. They found ways of hiding their copies of the Scriptures so that they could be safe from search. They hid them in rice-pits or in holes dug in the floor of their huts, while other copies were hidden in caves and under rocky ledges far distant from their villages.

At last the complete Bible was printed and copies were bound. About seventy bound Bibles were left with the Christians. One man, hearing that Bibles were available, walked, even though he was in a feeble state of health, 100 miles to obtain his copy, which he received with tears of joy. The missionaries left copies of Psalms, Testaments and hymn-books with the Christians and a number of books were buried for greater security.

The missionaries had now done all they could, so in July 1836 David Johns and Edward Baker commended their brethren to the Lord and sorrowfully set out for the coast and for England. A few of the missionaries settled in Mauritius, where they would be near enough to help and encourage the believers as opportunity offered. From there David Johns made several visits to the east coast of Madagascar and was able to make contact with some of the believers from time to time. But opportunities of this sort were very limited. The missionaries may well have said, as Paul said to the Ephesian elders, 'We commit you to God, and to the word of his grace, which can build you up' (Acts 20:32). From now on, the Malagasy believers were largely left on their own. But they had the Bible in their hands and it is evident that they read and studied it, expounded and preached it, so that it became not only manna to the souls of the small company of believers then in existence, but a means of conversion and blessing to hundreds of their fellow countrymen in the years to come.

David Jones, the pioneer of the missionary band and the chief translator of the Bible, had returned to England, broken in health, in 1831. Even the queen had acknowledged his qualities and his great service to Madagascar. She had sent him a gracious letter of thanks and provided a guard of honour to escort him to the coast. But he could not remain in Britain. Six years later he sailed for Mauritius, somewhat improved in health. Finally, in 1840, he was able to visit Antananarivo in company with Lieutenant Campbell, who had come from Mauritius on what proved to be a vain mission intended to improve relations with Queen Ranavalona.[1] His schools were closed and all his work seemed to have come to nothing. But though his Malagasy friends dare not recognize him openly he did hear of their faith and courage in their trials. Nine Christians were put to death while he was there. He returned to Mauritius and died there in 1841. He did not live to see the triumph of the gospel he had proclaimed, but he did witness the steadfastness of the Christian believers.

Street in Toamasina

6.
The translation of the Bible

The Bible in their own language played a very large part in the survival of the Malagasy Christians under the fierce persecution they were about to endure. This fact can too easily be taken for granted. The faith which David Jones and his colleagues proclaimed in Madagascar during the fifteen years they were permitted to remain was not just the faith of the missionaries nor of the society which had sent them out; it was the faith set forth and declared in Holy Scripture. Thus the subsequent absence of the missionaries was regrettable but not disastrous. The Bible in the hands of the Christian believers themselves was the decisive factor.

But we may well ask how it was possible for these young

men to come to a land and people without a Bible and without even a written language, and to translate the whole of the Bible into their language and print it in such a short space of time. They first reduced the language of the Malagasy people to writing, unravelled the intricacies of its grammar and syntax and then made available to the Christians several hundred copies of the Scriptures in their own language. And all this within the space of fifteen short years! This was a prodigious undertaking, almost without parallel in the annals of missionary enterprise. How was this done? What aids did they have? What equipment of heart and mind did they bring to their task? And what was it which drove the missionaries to complete this task at the expense of other duties? Even in the days of King Radama's friendship and encouragement the translation of the Scriptures took precedence over all else and was pressed forward with the utmost vigour. It was almost as though they had a feeling even then that their time was limited.

First of all they recognized that the gospel could only make headway as the people had the Scriptures in a form they could understand. The L.M.S. was a new mission, founded only in 1795, and it was an expression of the new forward movement which was renewing and awakening the Christians of the British Isles, causing them to remember anew their Lord's command to take the gospel to all nations. It is easy to point up the shortcomings of the early nineteenth-century missionaries – their long frock coats and heavy ankle-length dresses and their ignorance of anthropology. But certain principles were clear to them. They went with the gospel of Jesus Christ to peoples who did not know of him, and they knew that that gospel was embodied in Holy Scripture. So we find that with the beginning of the missionary movement there was also another movement, the urge to translate the Scriptures into a host of languages hitherto unknown. There were dire predictions of the imprudence and even the certain failure of these attempts to make the Word of God known 'indiscriminately to all', but nevertheless the missionary translators pressed on. Before the end of the eighteenth century William Carey had begun his great work of translation in India. The Reverend Henry Martyn sailed to that same land in 1805, and by the time he

The translation of the Bible

died seven years later he had done valuable translation work in Hindustani and Arabic and had translated the New Testament into Persian. At about the same time Robert Morrison was translating the Bible into the Chinese language. Many similar instances could be quoted – in Burma, in the Pacific Islands and elsewhere. All of these activities were helped and funded in various ways by the newly formed British and Foreign Bible Society.

In the same way, and moved by the same impulse, David Jones and his co-workers began at once to give the Malagasy people the Scriptures in their own language. They preached, they taught school, they imparted trade skills in timber and brick, but above all they gave themselves to the translation of the Scriptures. It had not always been so. Missionary enterprise of earlier times had not shown the same zeal for Bible translation. In 1643 a French company had established a trading post and a Christian mission at Fort Dauphin, in the extreme south of the island. By the year 1657 Sieur Etienne de Flacourt, one of the principals of the mission, had produced a catechism and the Lord's Prayer in Malagasy. It appears that at the same time a considerable number of Malagasy words and phrases were transcribed and written down. But no Scripture translation was attempted and no attempt was made to provide the people with the Word of God, although many thousands of Malagasy were baptized into the Catholic faith. Troubles soon beset the new colony, and within a few years trading post and mission were no more, and almost all trace of the work disappeared.

A further attempt along similar lines was made more than a century later. In 1768 the Count de Maudave brought an expedition to Fort Dauphin with the object of setting up a new colony. The venture only lasted two and a half years and was then abandoned. Perhaps as a result of this venture a book was published in France in 1785, the author of which is unknown. It contains a catechism and the Lord's Prayer translated into Malagasy. Both this and the earlier work referred to above are very difficult to read, and it is doubtful whether many Malagasy would have been able to comprehend them. But these and other efforts along similar lines were all brave attempts to give the Malagasy people a written language. Their authors did not wholly succeed in their task, but they did pioneer the way, and some of their efforts may well have indicated to David Jones and his colleagues how *not* to tackle the task. The great weakness of all these early experiments was that there was no consistency in the matching of sounds to letters. The same Malagasy sound was rendered in a dozen different ways, making the reading of the words difficult and at times impossible. It seems also that very few Malagasy were taught to read their own language. It was to be left to the Welsh missionaries to produce a workable transcription of the Malagasy language into writing.

In 1812 the Governor of Mauritius, Robert Farquhar, had attempted the translation of the Gospels into the Malagasy language. He seems to have had as his helper one or more of the Malagasy people in Mauritius. He desisted in his efforts after a time, feeling that the task ought to be undertaken by Christian missionaries, such as those of the London Missionary Society. Not only in Mauritius but in Madagascar itself there were tentative efforts to write down the Malagasy language. King Radama was learning French and a book of exercises in his own handwriting exists to this day. At the same time there were some Arab people at his court, and they were attempting to write down the Malagasy language in their own Arabic script.

The year 1818, as we have seen, saw the arrival of the first Protestant missionaries to Madagascar. Would they do any better than their predecessors? Would they succeed where the others had failed? It was evident that David Jones was himself not ill-equipped for the task of Bible translation. He was at home in his own Welsh tongue and in English. At the L.M.S. training college at Gosport he had studied Greek and Hebrew. There the need to learn the native language had been impressed upon him and upon all the students. He had also studied Persian and Malay. While still in Mauritius he had begun the study of Arabic, having heard in 1817 that some Malagasy could read and write in the Arabic script. Furthermore, when he set out for Madagascar the famous Dr Johnson had not long completed his dictionary of the English language. (He died on 13 December 1784.) Dr Johnson's comments about the spelling of the English

The translation of the Bible

language had some influence on David Jones' approach to the question of Malagasy orthography. He saw the need for a simpler and more consistent spelling than we have in English.

All this background information and other material were available to Jones and Bevan as soon as they set foot in Mauritius in 1818. They lost no time in making use of it, and were no doubt able to begin a study of the Malagasy language almost at once. Charles Telfair, secretary to Governor Farquhar, in writing to the L.M.S. in London in 1820, said that 'The voluminous mass of MSS on the language of the Island, written by the Catholic missionaries in former days, have been deeply studied by Mr Jones, and his progress has been proportionally rapid.'[1] By the end of the first year Jones and Bevan had already fixed the broad outlines of the Malagasy alphabet. When David Jones returned alone to Mauritius in 1819, after the tragic end of the first attempt to begin a work in Madagascar, he threw himself into the work with renewed vigour and it seems that by 1820 he had completed a translation of the Gospel of John into the Malagasy language.

However, the way of representing some sounds had still to be decided and in fact it was not till 1828 that all points were settled and an alphabet of twenty-one letters agreed upon. This meant that the missionaries had to revise the spelling of much of the vocabulary they had already collected. As a result of their labours the written language flows easily and is not difficult to read. In general the English pronunciation of the consonants was followed, the vowels on the other hand being French or Italian in sound. The Malagasy language does not use the letters 'c, q, u, w' and 'x'. The 'o' is sounded 'oo' as in 'moo' and the 'j' has the sound of 'dz'. The 'y' is used in place of 'i' at the end of a word, and has the same value. It is pronounced 'ea' as in 'tea', so the Malagasy word *tia* is pronounced 'tea-a'. King Radama had his say too about the written language of his people, based no doubt on his study of the French language and of the written Arabic script which had been exhibited before him. He insisted that there should be one value or one sound for each letter throughout, something which the missionaries had already agreed on. He also declared

An open-air market on the Pangalene Channel in the Toamasina region

emphatically for the Roman alphabet as against the Arabic, because he saw how much simpler it was.

It may perhaps seem boring to modern readers to consider the Malagasy alphabet, but it was a matter of immense importance at the time, and on the whole the early translators did a good job. Their work has been criticized, as for instance in the works of William Ellis, a historian of the period. He said that the 'oo' sound (as in *Hova*, pronounced Hoover) should have been spelt 'u', (so that *Hova* would have been *Huva*, and so on). But the language was written for the benefit of the Malagasy themselves, not for others. The form of the language in which Jones and his colleagues worked is the Hova dialect, spoken in Imerina, the central part of the island. As Hova soldiers, and later Hova traders, moved about in every corner of the island, so the Hova dialect became the standard written language of Madagascar. The Malagasy all speak one language, from Diego-Suarez in the north to Fort Dauphin, but there are many differences in vocabulary and pronunciation. It remains true, however, that the Hova dialect, being the most widely spoken, was and still is the most suitable form of the language for the translation of the Scriptures.

Building on the work of his predecessors, David Jones had reduced the language of the Malagasy people to writing in a form which would enable him, and the Malagasy people themselves, to read and write it with ease. The written language is only a tool, and David had no doubts as to how that tool was to be used. It was first of all to give the people the Bible in their own tongue. He began by opening a school. But if schoolteacher by day he was translator by night, and slowly the written Malagasy Bible began to appear. After a time he was joined by David Griffiths, who shared his vision.

Within five years of Jones's arrival at the capital the missionaries were able to use the brightest of their pupils to translate verses of Scripture from English into Malagasy. David Griffiths even had visions of these Malagasy youths undertaking Greek and Hebrew studies in order to assist in the translation.

But with or without such assistance the missionaries were proceeding apace with their task. In August 1825 Jones wrote, 'Having finished the translation of the N.T. we proceed with that of the Old this year as diligently as other affairs of the mission will allow us to attend to it.' In April of the following year Griffiths was able to write, 'A version of the Scriptures is rendered into the Malagasy language, and we now go on as fast as possible with revising our translation.' By 1828 they were able to say that the translation had been revised and re-revised.

As indicated above, some of the more advanced pupils had a share in the work. It appears they were employed chiefly to check the completed Malagasy translation with the English Bible. Later on, when the book had reached the printing stage, young men and women were employed in sewing and binding the completed copies and were paid wages for the work done. In the first instance these young men were chosen by King Radama and were paid a government salary. Strangely enough, when Queen Ranavalona succeeded him she continued the arrangement and even conferred an honour on each of those who were engaged in the work. Concerning the translation itself, missionaries of a later generation had nothing but praise for the work done. Mr W.E. Cousins, who directed the revision of the Malagasy Bible in the years 1873–1887, declared, in a somewhat back-handed compliment that 'The work was not performed in a careless or perfunctory manner.' The Rev. James Sibree, who came to Madagascar in 1863, described the translation as 'wonderfully correct and idiomatic'. But the true worth of the work done is seen in the lives of those who nourished their spirits on its words in their time of persecution.

In 1820 a printing-press had been sent out from England. But, alas, Charles Hovenden the printer, who arrived with the press, succumbed to fever and died within six weeks of his arrival! Here was a set-back indeed: the new press still in its packing cases, the printer dead, and no qualified printer on the staff of the mission. Eventually, however, the press was unpacked and set up. For by this time James Cameron had arrived, and while he was not a printer he had had experience with machinery. A handbook found with the machinery was a very great help, and to that was added James Cameron's natural aptitude with anything mechan-

The translation of the Bible

ical. So with Cameron's expertise the press could be assembled, and it was. David Jones then took over. He had worked for a few months at a printing-press, and so was able to put his small skill to good use. The first experimental page produced on the new press was Genesis 1:1–23. It was a great day for the mission and for the gospel enterprise in Madagascar. The serious work of Bible publication could now begin. The missionaries dedicated the year 1828 by beginning on 1 January the printing of the Gospel of Luke. The New Testament was now begun in earnest. The British and Foreign Bible Society made several gifts of paper for this project.

There were a number of problems with the press, which was constructed of wood. The missionaries made an urgent request to London for a metal press to replace it, but the new press did not arrive until 1834 and was in fact never put to use. The wooden press had to be repaired from time to time. At some point the stone platen was broken and the printers had to improvise. Of all the difficulties which beset the missionaries not the least was this inadequate and over-worked wooden printing-press. Edward Baker, the second printer, who arrived towards the end of 1828, referred in a letter home to their 'most inefficient and crazy printing department'. Another problem was due to shortages in the movable type. Due to the peculiarities of the Malagasy language, which has an abundance of vowels, they were constantly short of type, and could only set up limited amounts of work at one time. Nevertheless the work went ahead and the New Testament was completed in February 1830. There was a great demand for this first edition of the New Testament. Distribution was free: the mission made no charge for copies of the book since most of the people were considered too poor to be able to buy their own copy. It was given to all classes – soldiers, officers, schoolchildren, women and to the young men in Mr Chick's workshop. By August 1830 about 425 New Testaments had been distributed.

As already indicated, the Old Testament had already been translated by the time the New Testament was printed. The time was now short, the clouds were gathering and the menacing storm seemed about to break. Ever since her accession to the throne in 1828 Queen Ranavalona had shown her hatred and opposition to the Christian faith. She valued the missionaries for their contribution in the way of book-learning, for the skills they taught in woodwork, metalwork, leather-work and so on, although she opposed the gospel implacably. She therefore permitted the missionaries to stay on in the hope that they might be able to teach new skills to her people. Thus a valuable respite was gained and the missionaries were able to complete the printing and binding of the whole Bible before they were finally compelled to leave the country. The queen's desire to squeeze the last ounce of artisan skill out of the missionaries enabled them to make available to their converts the priceless treasure of the Word of God.

By the year 1836 only two missionaries remained in Antananarivo: David Johns and Edward Baker. Before departing for Mauritius in July 1836 Johns and Baker left for the Christians 'about seventy complete Bibles and several boxes of Psalters, Testaments, Spelling and Hymn books, Catechisms and Tracts', most of which were buried in the ground for greater security.

The great and enduring legacy of fifteen years' work was the Bible, the living Word of God, in the language of the people and in the hands of the Malagasy Christians. We may not dismiss as of little consequence the other work accomplished in that time – the thousands of pupils in the numerous schools throughout Imerina, the skills taught and acquired in a variety of arts and crafts. These were all useful in their way and paved the way for the greater and more important task. For these activities, far from hindering the main task, helped to make it possible and to bring it to completion. But above all, all praise is due to Almighty God for the sense of urgency imparted to the missionaries which meant that their highest priority was always the translation of the Scriptures. In the providence of God this task was completed. It remains for us to see the place the Bible had in the lives of the little band of believers left to face the persecution in 1835 and in the following twenty-five years.

The spearing of the first martyr

7.
The storm breaks out afresh

We have met already in our story the man and his wife who went to purchase an idol and who had the words of Isaiah chapter 44 read to them a few days afterwards. This lady had been one of the most ardent supporters of idol-worship, but when confronted with the scripture which spoke so strongly of the folly of idol-worship she became a Christian, and was henceforth as zealous and bold for the Lord as she had previously been for the empty worship of idols. Her name was Ra-fára-vávy and at her baptism she took the name of Mary and was then known as Rafaravavy Mary. She purchased one of the largest houses available in the capital so that she might use it as a place for prayer and preaching.

This had all taken place before the suppression of Christianity.

Just before the last two missionaries had quitted the capital, on 17 July 1836, three of Rafaravavy's servants went to denounce her to the judge. She and nine of her friends, they said, continued to pray and to read the Scriptures. Word was brought to her of the accusation and she immediately took her Bible and other books to the missionary for safe keeping. When her father heard what the slaves had done he had them put in irons. Rafaravavy, however, had them released, sent for them and spoke to them with tears of the forgiveness and mercy of God in Christ. Two of these slaves afterwards became Christians.

Rafaravavy refused to disclose the names of her companions. The queen was very angry when she learned of her offence and ordered that she be put to death at once. However, she was pardoned on account of the services rendered to the state by her father and brother and was ordered to pay a fine. She was warned that the penalty for a further offence would be death. As she found herself constantly watched and spied on, she bought a house at Ambatonakanga, and there a small company of believers met from time to time for prayer. Occasionally they travelled twenty miles or more in order to hold their meetings in greater security; sometimes even on top of a mountain, where they could sing and pray more freely.

About twelve months after his departure David Johns visited the coast and met with four of the Christians, who gave him news of their friends in the interior. The queen, they said, had not relented at all as regards the Christian gospel. She thought that, without the support of the missionaries, the people would soon forget the teaching. 'But,' they said, 'the queen does not know that the best Teacher of all, the Holy Spirit, is still with us.'

Meanwhile, in Antananarivo, the enemies of the Christians were still active in seeking their condemnation. A relative of one of the Christians accused them of meeting with Rafaravavy at her house for prayer. Rafaravavy was sent for and commanded to declare the names of her companions. She was questioned repeatedly and the officers told her that the queen knew the names of her companions but that her penalty would be reduced if she confessed who they were. But her reply was: 'If the queen knows who they are, why do you ask me again?' Then one of Rafaravavy's companions was brought before her. She said, 'Yes, we have prayed, we do not deny it.' When questioned further she replied that they had prayed in many places: in the house and out of doors, in the town and in the country; wherever they went they endeavoured to remember their God and to pray to him.

There were some Christians already in prison, and these were questioned in order to induce them to name others who had not yet been accused. One young woman, Rá-sa-láma by name, was falsely told that the names of all the Christians were known to the government. Rasalama was thus trapped into revealing the names of seven other believers, among whom was Paul the Diviner. These were all immediately arrested and details of their names and the charges against them were brought to the queen. When questioned Paul replied that he had indeed prayed to God who created him and who supported him. He prayed that God would make him a good man, that he would bless the queen, the officers and the judges and would make them wise and good. It is no wonder that there were many who said there was no evil, but only good, in such praying. But the reply was that the queen had forbidden anyone to pray to Jehovah and to Jesus, so they were guilty.

Of all the ways in which Christian believers may be described, among the Malagasy they were described as those who prayed. Perhaps it tells us something about these early Christian believers in Madagascar, that they did not merely *confess* the name of Jesus, but that they were known as those who *prayed* to him. Their faith, from the beginning, was not a matter of belief or custom, but the faith of those who called upon the name of the Lord in prayer. So they were asked time and again, 'Do you pray?' An affirmative answer was sufficient to label them as believers in Christ.

Rafaravavy Mary was considered to be the leader of the Christians and her death was determined by the government. Her property was forfeited and the first intimation she had of that was a crowd of people rushing to her house from the market to seize her property and even to pull down the building itself. She herself was led along towards Am-bóhi-pótsy, at the southern end of the city, where criminals were usually put to death. It seemed that her death was very near. She prayed, like Stephen, for forgiveness for her executioners. A fellow Christian accompanied her in order to strengthen her in her last hour. They stayed overnight at a house belonging to one of the officers. Heavy fetters were riveted onto her limbs and she heard she was to be executed on the morrow at cock-crow. But at midnight a great fire broke out in the capital, the fire spreading along the thatched roofs of the houses. A strong wind increased the destruction and a great deal of confusion and panic were caused. An order was issued suspending all government service. This meant that Rafaravavy's execution could not proceed until further orders. Thus her life was preserved for the present, causing one person to exclaim, 'God is indeed the Sovereign of life!'

Paul and Rafaravavy were kept in irons in separate houses. Others were still held prisoner and the queen threatened death or slavery to all who continued praying. Rasalama was still held captive and was led to see that she had been the cause of some of her companions being apprehended. The beatings and ill-treatment she had received had seemed to unsettle her mind, but this was only for a short time. Her courage revived and she declared that she rejoiced to be counted worthy to suffer for Jesus. Her execution was ordered and she was bound in heavy fetters, made in such a way as to cause great suffering to the wearer. She said, 'You say Rafaravavy will be put to death; but no, she will not die. I will be killed instead of her.'

And so it came about. Next morning Rasalama was led up the long climb to the place of execution. On the way she sang hymns of praise to her Lord and on reaching the fateful spot she asked leave to pray, which was granted. Then she fell, with the spears of the executioners in her body. There were those standing by who taunted the Christians, asking, 'Where is the God she prayed to, for he does not save her?' But the executioners repeatedly said that there is surely some charm in the religion of the white people which takes away the fear of death. One young man, Ra-fára-láhy by name, was standing by when Rasalama was killed, and he

The storm breaks out afresh

exclaimed that if he could die so tranquil a death he too would willingly die for the Saviour. So died Rasalama, a young woman, young also in the faith, who became the first martyr for Jesus Christ in Madagascar. She was the first, for there were to be many others who would esteem their love for their Lord greater than life itself. Rasalama died on 14 August 1837.

The other Christians who had been apprehended, some 200 altogether, were all sold into slavery. The aged Paul the Diviner, who had been kept in heavy irons day and night, became a slave of the chief minister. He and the other Christian slaves were sent into the rice fields to work, but at night they had a hut to themselves, where Paul was a great strength and comfort to his fellow sufferers.

Rafaravavy had been kept in irons for some months, under constant guard. Then she was sold in the public market to the chief military officer. She was in the charge of one of his aides-de-camp and he treated her kindly and gave her liberty to come and go. She was also able to spend time with her husband, a colonel in the army, who had obtained leave and was able to be with her. From time to time she was able to meet with fellow Christians at the home of Rafaralahy, the young man who had accompanied Rasalama to her execution. Rafaralahy's house was in a secluded place, to enable the Christians to meet in safety. This young man was most zealous to spread the knowledge of the Saviour and he spoke to many about the way of salvation. He was most concerned for his mother and asked many to pray for her that she might come to a knowledge of the truth.

He had a companion, who professed also to be very zealous for the faith. This man complained of poverty so Rafaralahy took him into partnership. But he lost some of the goods, or pretended to, and thus got into Rafaralahy's debt. When asked for payment he went at once to the officers and betrayed his friend, disclosing that Rafaralahy was holding meetings for Christians in his house. Rafaralahy was arrested and put in irons, but refused to reveal the names of his companions. He simply replied, 'I am here; I have done it. Let the queen do as she pleases with me; I will not betray my friends.' He was confined in heavy irons for three days and then led away for execution, to the very spot where he had witnessed the death of Rasalama nearly twelve months before. On the way to his execution he spoke to the soldiers of the love and mercy of Christ. He spent his last moments in prayer and then quietly yielded his body to the spears of the executioners. He was only twenty-two years of age.

Rafaralahy's wife was a timid woman, whom the Christians regarded as a believer in Christ. She and one of her husband's Christian companions were seized and were severely tortured and threatened until they revealed the names of those who had met with Rafaralahy to read the Scriptures and to pray in his house. They were unable to hold out against the barbaric treatment they suffered and they gave the names of Paul, of Rafaravavy Mary and several others. For the first two, to be arrested would mean certain death.

Events had happened so quickly that the news of the death of Rafaralahy and the arrest of his widow was not yet generally known. At this very time Rafaravavy, with two other Christian women, was in the home of a friend not far away. Suddenly a slave entered the house and gave a note to Rafaravavy. It told of the death of Rafaralahy and of the disclosure of her name by his wife. The three women left the house and set out at once for the capital. At the foot of the hill they knelt together in prayer and then parted, expecting only to meet each other again in heaven. Rafaravavy had no thought then of trying to escape. She was hurrying to the house of her master, for she preferred to be arrested there and not at the house of a friend. Her two friends fled to a distant part of the country and were not heard of again for some time.

Rafaravavy entered the city and as she hurried along she was called by a group of Christians, including David and Simeon. From them she received confirmation of the death of Rafaralahy. They tried to find Paul and others in order to advise them of their peril. After much consideration and prayer together they decided it was their duty to save their lives if they could, rather than just give themselves up. In this decision they were guided not by mere human prudence, but rather by what they believed the Lord would have them do. Rafaravavy and her friends had entered the

The storm breaks out afresh

city fully expecting to be apprehended and executed. But the conviction was borne upon them that they should flee for their lives.

At midnight Joseph, David and his wife, Andría-nimánana and Rafaravavy left the city. There were watchmen, but they thought the Christians were members of a party returning to the country after fetching timber for the government, so they allowed them to proceed. They were not a moment too soon. A warrant had been issued for the arrest of Rafaravavy, and next day she was sought for throughout the city, but without success. It had not been possible to warn Paul the Diviner, so he was arrested, along with Rafaravavy's nephew, and both were put in irons. It was decided not to kill them until Rafaravavy too was in the hands of the government. It was thought that to execute four Christian leaders at once would strike terror into the hearts of all the Christians.

Before leaving the city two of the company had spent their last hours making up their accounts and leaving goods and money neatly packaged for their masters. For, having been sold into slavery, they had been employed in a trading venture, but they did not consider that the goods and money with which they had been entrusted were their own. When the packages containing money and cloth were discovered some months later their master was most astonished, and said, 'This is not the general custom of slaves who run away from their masters. These people would make excellent servants if they would but leave off their praying.'

The five fugitives fled to the west, and by the following evening they had travelled forty miles, to a village where friends gladly received them. For some three months they moved around from place to place, being supplied with food by friends. They thought of fleeing to the Sakalava country, but as the Sakalava were enemies of the Hova, they feared they would be put to death. Besides, the road to the Sakalava territory was through desert country and they could well have died of famine.

It is not possible to enumerate in detail the adventures and hardships and sufferings of this small group of Christians over the next few months. They were eagerly hunted by the queen's soldiers, who were often hot on their track. At the same time there was always the danger of being betrayed. They suffered hunger; they were drenched by the fierce tropical downpours; they slept among boulders, or on the flat tops of ancient tombs, and were in constant danger from brigands and robbers. But everywhere there were Christian friends ready to risk their lives to shelter them. The gospel had spread far from the capital and there were Christian believers in many villages, both near and far. But for Rafaravavy in particular the prospect seemed to be constant flight and imminent danger both day and night. It was for her the soldiers searched in village after village with a zeal and diligence worthy of a better cause.

David Johns, the last missionary to have left Antananarivo, was now at Toamasina on the east coast. He was prepared to arrange Rafaravavy's escape from Madagascar altogether, along with that of some others whose lives were forfeit to the queen's anger. Rafaravavy and her friends returned to Antananarivo, where they obtained food and shelter, and then, having received from Toamasina a message bidding them proceed, they set out on the long and dangerous journey to the coast. There was hardship and danger along every mile of the steep and slippery track through the forest from the high central plateau to the coast. They endured hunger and exhaustion and bore the cold and wet of the forest with its constant rain, while every moment they had to be on the alert against soldiers and spies. But at long last the party of five reached Toamasina and embarked on a ship for Mauritius. All five had been the objects of a long and diligent search by the queen and her officers. It was not David Johns who had urged that they escape from the island. The Christians themselves had felt it right in the sight of God to flee from their persecutors, they had appealed to the missionary for help and he had willingly risked much to assist them.

It appears there were seven who took ship and embarked for Mauritius: Rafaravavy Mary, Razafy Sarah, David Ratsarahomba, Simeon Andrianomanana and Joseph Rasoamaka, the five who had journeyed down from the capital, while Andrianilaina, husband of Sarah, and James

Andrianisa joined them at Toamasina. Andrianilaina remained in Mauritius, with the hope that he might return and help his fellow Christians. The others journeyed first to Cape Town, and then to England, funds having been raised by well-wishers to cover the cost of their fares. In England they were welcomed by friends and supporters of the London Missionary Society at a great meeting at Exeter Hall in London in May 1839. A great deal of sympathy and prayerful support was kindled for their suffering brethren still in Madagascar. They remained in England until 1842, and then they returned to Mauritius, except for one of their number, Razafy Sarah, who had died in England in 1841.

These people, who endured so much in travel and hardship in hiding and in their eventual escape to England, did not act without reason or according to their own whim. It is interesting to see their dependence all along on the Lord whom they served and their close attention to the message of his Word. A letter written by Rafaravavy to David Johns at Toamasina is full of quotations from Scripture. An extract from her letter will help us to see how completely she and her companions had learned to trust in God and to apply his Word to their own situation. She wrote: 'Health and happiness to you, beloved friend. May you enjoy with your family the blessing of God, and all the missionaries who have been with us, and the congregations where you dwell. As to things here and the state of our relatives, wickedness is on the increase, and opposition too. They are now continually saying, "You will be arrested by the Tsi-tia-lainga. You are not afraid of the sovereign; you are doing what she has forbidden". . . I rejoice that this has happened to me. It brings to my remembrance Acts 14:22; 2 Tim. 3:12. Blessed be God who has given us access through Jesus Christ. May he enable me to obey the words of Jesus to his disciples, "If anyone will come after me, let him deny himself, etc." None of these things move me, neither count I my life dear to myself that I may finish my course with joy. I exhort you not to grieve, for your labour has not been in vain in the Lord. The number of converts is increasing. If our gospel be hid, it is hid to them that are lost, but it is the power of God to salvation to them that are saved. Therefore

I take confidence. The power of God cannot be hindered ... Pray for us – may God open a door for his Word among us, 2 Thess. 3:1, 2.'

When Rafaravavy first returned to Antananarivo, after learning that her name had been revealed as one who still kept up praying, she and her friends had no thought of fleeing to save themselves. Then they remembered that David had fled from Saul when the latter sought his life. And they remembered too the words of the Saviour to his disciples: 'When you are persecuted in one place, flee to another' (Matt. 10:23). On one occasion Rafaravavy was in the home of a Christian couple in a village some distance away. A band of soldiers was making a thorough search in every village and in every house for her and her companions. As they sat together in the small house the lady of the house heard the noise of crows and went to the door to see if they were eating the rice which was spread out in the courtyard. Looking out, she saw two soldiers approaching the house with spears in their hands. She whispered to Rafaravavy, who went quickly into the other room and hid herself under the bed, rolled in a mat. The soldiers entered the house and searched everywhere, enquiring at the same time whether the couple had seen Rafaravavy. They countered the enquiries by asking which Rafaravavy the soldiers meant. The men remained about an hour, with just a thin partition between them and her hiding-place. She was alarmed at first and breathed so hard she thought they must surely hear her. She committed herself to God; then there came to her mind a most suitable verse of Scripture:

> 'Have no fear of sudden disaster
>   or of the ruin that overtakes the wicked,
> for the Lord will be your confidence
>   and will keep your foot from being snared'
>
>   (Prov. 3:25–6).

She remembered also how the Lord had preserved David from Saul in the cave, so she took courage and was calm. Many similar instances could be cited. These Christians in Madagascar, deprived of the teachings of the missionaries, had learned to stay their souls on the promises of God and on the power of his Word.

In the meantime the rage of the persecutors of the Christians continued. A very attractive young lady named Rá-vahíny had been divorced by her husband because of her faith in Christ. She had been sold into slavery and had been repudiated by her father as well as by her husband. Some of her relatives arranged that she should be compelled to drink the *tangena*. She was made to do so and perished under its effects.

Three Christian women, all friends of Rafaravavy, were accused of meeting together for prayer. When the officer came to arrest them two of them were reading the Scriptures together. One escaped, but the other was apprehended and flogged most severely to force her to reveal the names of her companions. She was beaten that night and again in the morning until she fainted from pain and loss of blood. But she did not give her tormentors the satisfaction they sought. She was sold into slavery and was ordered to take the *tangena*, but escaped before it was administered. Her companions fled to an uninhabited part of the country and were never heard of again.

As the Christians were forced to flee to distant parts, so the gospel influence grew and increased. We have seen how Rafaravavy and her companions were forced to move from place to place over a period of several months, and how they were utterly dependent for food and shelter on the inhabitants of these distant villages. Yet in town after town they found Christian people ready to risk all to help them. Not all the Christians were known to the government and in any case the number of believers was continually increasing. The friendship of the Christians for one another was not explained by the ordinary courtesies of social life or by the natural hospitality of the Malagasy to strangers. Malagasy social life had its class system, from the princes and descendants of former kings, through the nobles and down to common workers and domestic slaves. Among the Christians, however, these class distinctions dissolved. Rafaravavy, as we have noted, was the wife of a colonel in the army and a high-born woman of property. Others who had become Christians were servants or even slaves. Their fellowship in Christ transcended all these class distinctions, binding them to one another in the firm bonds of the Saviour's love. When Rafaravavy and her companions travelled forty or fifty miles from home before seeking help or rest, they were received, sheltered and provided for by the local believers as if they had been their dearest relatives.

Consolation to a Christian in chains

8.
The persecution continues

Ever since Cain slew his brother Abel the Evil One has been trying to bring the work of God to nought and always he has failed. As Herod killed the infants of Bethlehem, so the Queen of Madagascar killed the disciples of Christ. As Herod failed in his purpose, so too did Queen Ranavalona fail in hers. It happened in Madagascar as it had happened long before when Pharaoh and his officers afflicted the people of Israel: 'The more they were oppressed, the more they multiplied and spread' (Exod. 1:12).

These Malagasy Christians were not protesting for the right to worship as they pleased, nor were they deliberately opposing the authority of the governing power in their land.

Their desire was to remain faithful to the Lord who had redeemed them. Their faith as Christians would make them better citizens of their country, and not rebels against it, as the queen supposed. They often prayed for their tormentors and even when being carried to the place of execution they spoke of the blessings of the gospel of Christ.

As the persecution continued, the great body of the people grew less willing to inform against the Christians. They dared not speak favourably of those who were being put to death, for that would be construed as treason, but the Christians gained the respect and pity of many of the populace. None could fail to mark the contrast between the meek uncomplaining submission of the Christians and the parade of power put forth by their executioners. The Rev. William Ellis visited Madagascar three times in the 1850s and he spoke to many of the Christians during these visits. They told him of their sufferings and fears and of the consolation of the gospel, but not once did he hear any expressions of anger or hatred against their persecutors.

Nevertheless the rage of the queen and the malice of their accusers bore heavily on the Christians. The order was given that the soldiers were to seek out and destroy all the Christians. In a letter sent to Mauritius they said, 'We have heard of the orders of the queen respecting us, and the manner in which we are to be put to death if discovered. We still confide in the compassion of the Saviour. Can you do anything to rescue us? The spirit is willing, but the flesh is weak.' Again they wrote, praying 'That if possible, you may do something to relieve us. We say, "if possible," for the Saviour prayed, "If it be possible, may this cup be taken from me."'

Some of the Christians were well known to the authorities. Paul the Diviner was declared innocent by the *tangena* and was set at liberty, together with one of his companions. But on hearing that he was to be put to death secretly he fled into hiding. Then towards the end of 1839 Joshua, a young man and a leader among the Christians, was discovered at prayer with eight others. They were threatened with the *tangena* and fled. They joined others who had been in hiding, some of them for up to two years. There were now sixteen of them. Some of the missionaries were

The persecution continues

still at Mauritius and word was sent that they would help the group escape from Madagascar if they could reach the coast. This seemed the only way to save their lives.

On 23 May 1840 the sixteen Christians began to make their way to Toamasina, led by two guides. Through a misplaced confidence they were discovered and captured and all sixteen were brought back to the capital for trial. When they were within a few miles of the city one young woman escaped and fled to the home of a friend, where she found refuge. The others were brought into the city and examined one by one. They were threatened and cajoled to reveal the names of their fellow believers, but though there were upwards of 200 Christians in Antananarivo at that time, they did not betray a single one.

The prisoners were then bound and confined in separate houses until sentence should be declared by the queen. In one house were two people, a young man and a young woman, bound separately and guarded by a soldier. The young man found he could loosen his cords with his teeth and he soon had his hands free, and then his feet. But the sleeping soldier was lying across the bonds of his companion, and he could do nothing to free her. He opened the window, found that the guard outside was also asleep, climbed out and, like Peter of old, fled to the home of his friends, who were astonished to see him.

On 9 July a *kabary* was held and the queen's sentence was declared. The Christians had continued to pray in spite of all she could do, and some of them had even tried to flee the country. Of the sixteen who were caught eleven were condemned to death, but of these two had escaped. The other nine were to be taken to the place of execution. Because of the extreme privations they had undergone they were too weak to walk, and so were carried, tied to poles, but naked. David Griffiths, the missionary, was in Antananarivo at the time, and so too was David Jones, in company with Lieut. Campbell. The victims were taken first to David Griffiths's house. In no way could he lift a finger to help them. Was David Jones, the pioneer missionary, also a witness of their sufferings? We do not know. In a letter to the L.M.S. David Jones wrote that David Griffiths and Lieut. Campbell were standing together on the balcony of

Mr Griffiths' house as the victims were led by.[1] It was reported that all seemed to be praying, and some wore expressions of serenity, even of hopeful joy, as they were carried to the place of execution. David Griffiths was accused of aiding the Christians in their flight. He was fined a total of thirty pounds and ordered to leave the country within a fortnight. The nine were brought to a rugged hill, known as Am-bóhi-jana-háry (the hill of God), and there they fell beneath the spears of the executioners. One of the nine was Paul the Diviner. His head and that of Joshua the preacher were struck off and fixed on poles as a warning to others.

The execution of these Christians brought no peace to the people nor strength to the government. The common people were oppressed, those in power were greedy for gain and armed brigands roamed the countryside. At the same time several hundred people were awaiting trial for various alleged offences. The queen's hand was heavy on all her subjects, and not only on those who had forsaken the idols and embraced the gospel of Christ. Nor was the anger of the persecutors appeased by these latest deaths. The believers were in danger in city and in country. They were less able to meet together for prayer than they had been previously, as their places of meeting were now more difficult of access, and fewer were able to attend them. The soldiers hunting for the Christians were more numerous and were coming to know their hiding-places. It was growing more difficult either to hide or flee. They had no earthly helpers and were bowed down by their afflictions. But their faith did not fail, even in this their darkest hour, and there were even additions to their numbers. The steadfastness of their faith and the evident care and presence of their Saviour were speaking to their fellow countrymen more clearly than the preached Word.

In Vonizongo, a district to the west, the Christians heard that the Sakalava chiefs on the north-west coast were willing to receive Christian teachers. Two men went to visit them. However, on their return they were arrested and sent for trial. They were executed and their heads were severed and fixed on poles. The courage they showed at their execution served to commend the gospel rather than to discourage others.

Soon afterwards someone fixed a paper on the wall of a house with the words of Matthew 23:13 underlined: 'Woe to

The persecution continues

you, teachers of the law and Pharisees, you hypocrites! You shut the kingdom of heaven in men's faces. You yourselves do not enter, nor will you let those enter who are trying to.' The Christians did not believe that any of their number were responsible for this act. The perpetrator was never discovered, but the queen was very angry and required the offender to give himself up within four days. If discovered he would be cut in pieces. As no one confessed, a Christian named Raharo and several others were arrested, though there was no proof that they were implicated in any way. Raharo was ordered to take the *tangena*, and under it he died. Two others were put to death and their bodies cut into small pieces and burned. Freeman and Johns record a similar incident in 1835, when a page of the New Testament, with these same words underlined, was found not far from the house of the first officer. No action was taken at that time, except for a diligent but unsuccessful search for the offender.

Help and succour came to the Christians at this time from an unexpected quarter. The queen's only son and the heir to the throne was a young prince named Rakóton-dradáma. Radama was the name of the former king, his supposed father, and Rakoto means 'young lad', so his name probably meant 'Radama's young boy'. He was at this time about sixteen years old. He came in touch with a Christian, one of the earliest converts, who was a fearless preacher of the gospel. This man spoke to the prince about the gospel and he became deeply impressed. There was renewed activity at this time; meetings were held and large crowds gathered. The prince was persuaded to attend some of these meetings and then he asked to be more fully instructed in the faith. He had his own separate house and so whenever he was free from other matters some Christians came to his house and explained the Scriptures to him. He also attended worship on Sunday whenever possible.

Before the end of the year an accusation was brought against the Christians for continuing to hold meetings for prayer. A list containing 100 names was brought to the prime minister. He found there the name of his aide-de-camp, who was also a relative of his. He destroyed the list and proceedings were taken against only twenty-one people.

Prince Rakotondradama pleaded with his mother for these Christians, and as a result none were sentenced to death. Nine of them were ordered to drink the *tangena*, under which one died. Five were sold into slavery, two escaped and the others were held in chains. There was much thankfulness among the Christians that so many lives had been spared.

The prime minister sent his nephew, whom he loved dearly, to the Christian meeting, with orders that he should write down the names of all those present. The nephew went, but told the Christians why he had come and advised them to go home at once. He returned to his uncle and, when asked for the list, said he had no names at all. The prime minister saw he had been disobeyed. 'You will lose your head,' he said, 'for you also are a Christian.' 'Yes, I am,' replied the young man. 'If you will, you may put me to death, but I must pray.' The prime minister paused, then said, 'No, you shall not die.' So once again the Christians were saved, this time by the courage of this young man.

These events had the effect of an increasing leniency being shown to the Christians. The years 1847 and 1848 were a time of rest and refreshment. Even those in chains found their conditions eased and finally their chains were taken off altogether. But even while they were still in chains their friends were able to visit them freely, and some of the soldiers who guarded them were converted to Christ.

The greatest need of the Christians was for books. Their Bibles, Testaments and Psalm books were worn out with use. They had been patched and recovered and resewn and the edges of the pages covered with stronger paper, while many books were soiled by dust or smoke or soot, due to the places in which they had been concealed. Some had copied out portions of Scripture so that there would be a few more to go round. It seems too that some Bibles and Testaments were broken up into sections, so that each company of believers would have at least some portion of the Scriptures. When the Rev. William Ellis visited Madagascar in 1854 he was able to smuggle in about 1500 New Testaments, but that day was as yet still

The persecution continues

a long way off. One of the treasured exhibits in the library of the Bible Society in Cambridge is a copy of the Malagasy Bible, bound in leather and very worn and dog-eared round the edges. It is one of the martyr Bibles, preserved to this day as a memorial of those events.

The two years of respite were only a preparation for yet more severe trials and in 1849 the heaviest storm of persecution yet endured fell upon the church. On 19 February 1849 two houses belonging to Prince Ramónja, which had been used as places of worship, were torn down and their material carried off as spoil. Prince Ramonja was a cousin of Prince Rakotondradama and the two young men had been friends since childhood. Ramonja had embraced the gospel and had proved to be an immense help to the Christians.

At the same time eleven Christians were seized and put in chains. A *kabary* was called, at which the queen declared, 'I have killed some, I have made some slaves till death, I have put some in long and heavy fetters, and still you continue that praying.' A week later the Christians were ordered to give themselves up. They were called to take the oath which recognized the idols. One replied in this way: 'I do not pray to wood and stones. Unto God alone do I pray, for he is great. He cannot have associates, or other gods.' Another, who was descended from one of the Hova kings, said, 'God has given none to be worshipped on earth, nor under heaven, except the Name of Jesus Christ.' Many others responded in a similar manner. Between 2000–3000 believers were apprehended at this time. They were offered life and liberty if they would deny the faith. Only a very few, who had occasionally associated with the Christians, took the easy way out. The vast majority remained true to their Lord.

One of those arrested at this time was a girl named Ranívo. She was only sixteen years of age. It was through the reading of a tract that she became a Christian and she used to worship in the house of Raínimiádana. She was described as a beautiful young girl, tall and with a thick head of hair. She came from a tribe or clan from which the kings and queens were descended, and the queen herself wanted her life to be spared. She had come forward as being one who prayed and was brought before the judges at Análakély. When asked, 'Do you pray to the twelve sovereigns and to the idols and to heaven and earth?' she boldly replied, 'I do not pray to any of these, for the idols are the work of men's hands and heaven is the throne of God and earth is his footstool.' They continued questioning her closely, but she stood firm. A great crowd of people witnessed this young girl's good confession. Her relatives came to her with tears pleading with her to agree with the queen and live. The crowd made sport of her and mocked her, but it was said that her face shone like the face of an angel. A bystander is reported to have said, 'Never since we were born did we ever see anyone whose face shone with such beauty.' The trial over, Ranivo and her companions were shut up in prison alone until the morning, when sentence was to be pronounced. They were left to commune with their Lord, while those of their brethren who were still free met to pray for them.

Eighteen of the condemned Christians were sentenced to death. Four of them were nobles, and by a refinement of hypocrisy the government, not wishing to shed the blood of those of noble birth, declared that they should be burnt alive at Faravóhitra, at the north end of the great hill on which the city was built. The other fourteen, being of inferior rank, were led to the top of the great rock outcrop at Am-pa-marínana, where they were to be cast over the edge to their death. Their wives and children were to be sold into slavery. 117 were condemned to labour in chains for life. Of them 105 submitted to public flogging. 64 others were heavily fined. Another group of 1,643 were fined for attending Christian worship. Prince Ramonja, who held high office in the army, was for the same offence fined 100 dollars and reduced to the rank of a common soldier. Others were fined or reduced in rank. The total number dealt with by fine, imprisonment or death was 2,000 people, or, by some computations, nearer to 3,000.

The sentences were immediately carried out, to the accompaniment of cannon fire, drums and martial music, all intended to terrify the prisoners. Those who were condemned to die began to sing hymns that spoke of the joy they would soon experience in the presence of their Saviour.

The persecution continues

Those who were led to Faravohitra prayed and praised God even in the flames. The falling rain more than once extinguished the flames, which had to be rekindled. One of the women at the stake had added to all her other sufferings the pains of childbirth. When her child was born it was callously thrust into the fire. Then a large rainbow appeared, taken by many as a sign of God's promise and faithfulness, but an object of terror to some of the spectators, who fled at the sight of it. The testimony of one who stayed to the end was 'They prayed as long as they had any life. Then they died; but softly, gently. Indeed, gentle was the going forth of their life, and astonished were all the people around that beheld the burning of them there.'

The other fourteen were taken through the crowds to the top of the rock of Ampamarinana, bound hand and foot with cords, wrapped in mats and then pushed or rolled over the sloping edge to the jagged rocks 150 feet below. They too went to their deaths with calmness and courage. Ranivo, the young girl whom the queen was anxious to save, was given opportunity to recant. She refused to take the oath which would set her free, saying she would follow her martyred friends. Her own family pleaded with her, but her purpose was unshaken. Then the executioner struck her on the face, drew her back from the edge and pushed her towards her family, saying, 'She is insane, take her away to her parents.'

The day after these executions, the fines in money and cattle which had been inflicted for minor offences were reduced by half, but even so the fines imposed were still high enough to reduce many to abject poverty. At the same time the whole of the non-Christian community, gathered then at the capital for these proceedings, were required to take the oath of allegiance to the sovereign and the idols before being permitted to return home.

A heavier penalty was inflicted on Prince Ramonja. Not only was he reduced to the rank of a common soldier, but he was treated with considerable hardship. The comfortable clothing to which he was accustomed was taken from him, and he was frequently appointed to night duty attired only in a thin shawl, or *lamba*, for covering in the cold of the winter nights. As a result of these privations, he was in poor health for the remainder of his life but he continued to be a faithful friend to the Christians. The prince royal, Rakotondradama, was powerless to do anything to help him or the others. He had been accused to the queen for reading the Scriptures and for attending the meetings of the Christians. But the queen only said, 'Oh, Rakoto is young; he does not know what is proper, and he is my only son!'

The Children's Memorial Church, Faravóhitra

9.
Andriambelo

God in his mercy raised up more than one among the persecuted Malagasy Christians to be a leader and a source of encouragement to them. One of these was Rafaravavy, who, before her escape to the coast and her voyage to England, had put her home and wealth at the disposal of her fellow Christians. In 1836 she had bought a house in the suburbs of Antananarivo and there many believers used to meet for prayer and fellowship. She was recognized as a leader among the Christians and was therefore singled out for pursuit by the authorities. As we saw earlier, she was arrested and sold into slavery and was twice condemned to death. After her visit to England, she returned to Mauritius, where she laboured on behalf of the Malagasy exiles there. In 1843 she worked for a short time at Nosy Mitsio on the west coast of Madagascar in company with Joseph Rasóamaka. She died in Mauritius in April 1848. She was referred to once as 'the saintly Rafaravavy', and she did indeed witness a good confession for her Saviour.

Another leader among the Christians was Paul the Diviner. Even when he was working as a slave in his master's rice fields he had continued to encourage and strengthen his fellow Christians. He was later freed, then rearrested and finally was speared to death and beheaded in 1840.

Thanks to these people, and to others who exercised a vital role of leadership in those early years, the little band of believers left behind by the missionaries had not disintegrated into a state of incoherence in the face of their persecutors. They could so easily have given way to their fears and been scattered.

As we have seen, there was a period of comparative peace and quiet during 1847 and 1848. Prisoners were freed and large numbers gathered to hear the preaching of the Word. The outbreak of persecution which took place in 1849, the fiercest so far, might well have demoralized the Christians completely. Up to 3,000 had been named as continuing to pray to Jesus, and of them some had suffered a horrible death, while many others were sold into perpetual slavery.

There was no knowing what was still in store for the believers. Some who had been leaders among them, including Rafaravavy and Paul, were no longer with them. Joseph, one of the better-known preachers, had been put to death. Prince Ramonja, who had protected and encouraged the believers, was himself now reduced in rank and disgraced. But God did not leave his people like sheep without a shepherd. In their hour of need he raised up faithful shepherds to lead them. Pastor Rabary, in his *Maritiora Malagasy*, gives a resumé of the situation in 1856. As well as listing the number of worshippers and church members in and around Antananarivo he gives the names of ten men who were pastors and a similar number who were preachers. One of the latter was Andria-mbélo. This man's name occurs frequently in all the accounts of the growth of the Christian church in the central province of Imerina. Both during the persecutions and in the era of growth and development which followed them Andriambelo played a useful and honourable part.

It was in about 1847 that Andriambelo first heard the gospel. He had never met any of the missionaries nor attended their schools. He was born, the youngest of nine children, in Ambátofótsy, a village about six or seven miles north of the capital. Although his family belonged to one of the twelve clans of the nobility, the *andríana*, they were very poor. He made a precarious living for himself selling soap by the roadside, but even so he was too poor to have his own stock, but sold as agent for another trader. When he first heard the gospel he took little notice, thinking it was a new thing which would soon be forgotten. He only gradually came to accept the truth of it. But in time he became convinced and began to attend the secret meetings of the Christians. He learned to read and gave himself with great earnestness to the study of the Scriptures. He and other young men began to meet regularly for prayer and for mutual encouragement. They even met in the daytime, disguising their devotions by the pretence of holding a noisy feast. The boldness with which they sang and prayed caused difficulties to their fellow Christians, who were sure their foolhardy actions would expose them to the queen's spies.

In February 1849 there began the great persecution which has already been described. Andriambelo was apprehended for having religious books and for teaching others to pray, but because of his youth he was not heavily sentenced. He was sold as a slave with the possibility of redemption. His relatives purchased his release. He continued his studies and his preaching and was baptized in December of that year.

His programme of preaching, teaching and encouragement would surely have taxed the strongest constitution. There must have been a great need for preachers and teachers after the executions of 1849. Not only were several of the leaders removed by death, but also many of the remaining believers were no doubt fearful and discouraged. Andriambelo's parish included many homes in the capital and several surrounding villages. His labours began on

Saturday evening, when he and many other Christians would meet together and spend the whole night in reading, praying, singing and in conversation. Just before daybreak they would remember their Lord in the Breaking of Bread. He would then spend the morning in visiting other houses in Antananarivo where there were Christians who were afraid to attend larger meetings, or who were only recent converts and were known to himself only. He would break bread with them and in the afternoon would go to other villages. Such activities taxed his energy and often by the end of the day he was so tired he found it difficult to keep awake, even as he walked along. He recalls one occasion when he nearly fell into a ditch.

He was not able to continue these activities unmolested. He became a marked man, being recognized as one of the leaders of the Christian community. Large rewards of cash and honours were offered to any who could effect his capture. He had to keep himself in close hiding, but even so he more than once barely escaped capture. Up to this time he was still visiting homes in the capital, but he used to disguise himself for greater security. The promised rewards for his capture were an incentive to many people to search continually for him.

Some of the events of these times sound like a spy story. He was passing the night once with Christian friends, and it was deemed safer for him to stay on the ground floor of the house. One of the occupants of the place was a half-crazed woman. When she saw a plate of rice and other food being taken downstairs she peeped through a crack in the floor and saw Andriambelo down below. Next morning she related that she had had a strange dream. She dreamed she had seen Andriambelo in the house. Fearing that the weak-minded woman would chatter and give him away, his friends quickly moved him to another hiding-place.

Soon afterwards he had an even closer shave, not once, but twice. He had stayed in Antananarivo in the hope that the search for him might slacken. Proceeding through one part of the city in disguise he saw two men talking. One said to the other, 'Why, there's Andriambelo!' 'What are you thinking of?' said his companion. 'Andriambelo dare not show his face here.' As they disputed he hurried on and got out of sight. Soon afterwards he was in another part of the town and someone said, 'There is Andriambelo.' 'No', said the other, 'it isn't him at all.'

The risk of capture was growing more serious, and his friends persuaded him he must leave Antananarivo altogether. He determined to retire to the wild and solitary district of Vonizongo, about thirty miles to the north. So quietly one morning he and a companion stole out of the city. This was in the month of July 1857. They parted near the village of Antainóka, about six miles out. He said goodbye to his friend and continued his dangerous journey alone. A deep yearning to see his mother came over him, and despite the hazard he determined to go to Ambátofótsy where she lived. But there was no rest or safety there. His relatives hid him in the thick bushes growing in the moat surrounding the village. That same day a message came from the queen to say Andriambelo was condemned to death, and all his property, 'even to the manure in the cattle-pen', was to be confiscated. His mother and sisters were seized on a charge of hiding a felon and were taken to Antananarivo. There they were forced to undergo the *tangena* ordeal, but in the mercy of God they survived and were set free.

The news of their arrest greatly troubled Andriambelo, and he said to his companion as he hid in another village, 'Let me go and give myself up. I cannot bear to think of the trouble I am bringing on my family.' But she persuaded him to commit himself and his cause, and the members of his family, to the good hand of God and to continue his journey in safety.

He travelled on alone and he found there was need for constant vigilance and that he dare not show himself openly. In one place to which he came he saw it was too risky to enter the village, so he hid in a nearby cave. One day as he lay in the cave he heard the voices of people above who were plucking grass. Something startled them and they fled away. Fearing that he might be discovered, he left the cave and crept into a deep narrow valley, where he lived during the daytime, returning at night to the cave. In the night he was startled by a wild cat springing on him. Next morning at dawn he left the cave and sought refuge among the dense shrubs in the ditch surrounding the village. His presence disturbed the fowls, which set up a loud cackling. Suspecting a wild cat in the ditch, the villagers began throwing stones and one struck him on the head. Fortunately he was not discovered and when things were quiet he stole back to the cave, where a Christian friend brought him food.

This 'cops and robbers' situation continued, and it requires some imagination for us to appreciate the constant strain, the sleepless nights and the narrow escapes that this servant of God endured. There was a price on his head because he dared to preach Christ, and though he found many Christian friends ready to shelter him, he knew there were others who made it their business to seek out Andriambelo and collect the reward for his capture. On one occasion he was overtaken by darkness and had to seek shelter for the night near the village of Ambohimanga. In the house, as he entered, he noticed a number of men who were hunting for wanted Christians and who had also put up there for the night. To back off would be to invite suspicion, so he coolly joined in the evening meal and lay down to sleep in the same room as the government spies. They were up early in the morning, urged on by the call, 'Get going, you fellows. We have to be up bright and early to catch these Christians.' Our hero feigned sleep until they had gone.

On another occasion he was actually seen and chased by a party of soldiers. He got well ahead and took refuge in the house of a friend. Some Malagasy houses have a broad plank, called a *héntona*, fixed a couple of feet below the ridge-pole. Andriambelo quickly climbed up and settled himself on this plank. But he gave himself up for lost when the soldiers actually entered the house where he was. They had not seen him, however, and they began to prepare a meal for themselves. Soon he experienced a new danger, for the smoke from the fire rose up to where he was and he had the greatest difficulty in restraining a fit of coughing. There was no chimney and the smoke made its way out through the gaps in the thatch. He managed to control himself until the meal was cooked and eaten and the soldiers were again on their way.

Finally he reached Vonizongo where he joined some other Christians. But there was still need for extreme caution. After the conclusion of what proved to be the last wave of persecution, in 1857, he decided to return to Antananarivo and throw himself on the mercy of Prince Rakotondradama. The Queen was now old and ill. All Andriambelo's possessions had been taken by the government. Even his wife had been given as wife to someone else. He began again to visit Christians in Antananarivo and he preached and taught in many houses.

During his visit to Madagascar in 1854 William Ellis had the opportunity of meeting Andriambelo and several other of the Christians at Toamasina, some of whom could speak a little English. 'I learned much from them respecting their past trials and present position. Among these were Andriambelo and others of their preachers. I was deeply impressed with the gentleness of the demeanour of the first-named preacher, his varied intelligence, great activity, and unremitting endeavours to strengthen the faith of his brethren, as well as to urge upon all to whom he could safely speak the claims of the Gospel, and the blessing attending its reception. Sincerity and earnest devotion to Christ appeared to be the distinguishing features of his character.'[1]

Andriambelo survived the persecutions. When the queen died in 1861 the dark cloud was lifted and Christians were free to worship openly. The next year, 1862, Andriambelo was chosen as pastor of what became the largest church in Antananarivo, at Am-pári-bé. During his time as pastor nearly 1,000 people were received into membership. He refused to accept any stipend and remained comparatively poor. He was a very mild and gentle man. The quality of his life as a Christian was known and respected by all. It is said that when he appeared drunken men slunk away in shame and quarrels ceased. The widow and the orphan, the sick and the dying found in him a friend and comforter, and the prodigal and sinner came to him for counsel and help. He was loved by all and was never known to speak ill of anyone. He was for many years one of the pastors of the palace church, and it was he who baptized and received into church membership the queens Ranavalona II and Ranavalona III. He experienced some physical and mental weakness towards the end of his life, but his love to the Saviour never weakened. He continued as pastor of Amparibe Church almost to the time of his death in 1904. During the latter half of the persecution and for many years after his was one of the greatest names in the Malagasy church, not because of his intellectual powers so much as his high moral and spiritual character and his zeal for the cause of Christ. In the providence of God some of his people were 'put to death by the sword', but Andriambelo was among those who 'escaped the edge of the sword', and who lived to bless and encourage many of his brethren.

Consolation to a Christian in chains

10.
Closing years of the persecution

After the conclusion of the outbreak of the great persecution in 1849 the Christians had something of a breathing-space for the next eight years. This is not to say that all persecution had ceased. The Christians were still being hunted, and every fortnight, at the parade of the military, the queen's orders for the arrest of the Christians were read out to the soldiers. A large number of Christian officers had been sent to hard labour quarrying and dressing stone to make a stone building. Then they were sentenced to drag heavy logs from the forest – the severest labour known in Madagascar. When their sentences expired the pagan party proposed that they should again be sentenced, but this was opposed by the prince royal and they were released.

The Christians were also now more circumspect in their actions and drew less attention to themselves than in the past. In Antananarivo they were right under the eye of the authorities, nevertheless their meetings were well attended and sometimes even those in chains were able to attend the gatherings. In the provinces the people enjoyed comparative freedom and the number of believers continued to increase. The Christians now numbered several thousand, and even in the capital there were seven houses where worship was regularly maintained.

Rainiharo, one of the chief ministers, and one who had been a powerful and cruel persecutor of the Christians, was now dead. His son, who succeeded him, was a friend of the Christians. He, as well as others in high office, often helped them with money and in other ways. Rakotondradama, the prince royal, and his cousin Ramonja spent large sums of money assisting the Christians. On one occasion Prince Rakoto went to a place where a number of Christians were confined. He set them all free and told their keeper that if he were called to account he was to say that the prince had set them free.

The queen was old and ill, but her hatred of the Christians and her oppression of the people in general did not abate, rather the reverse. On one occasion a young servant girl brought her a glass of water. She tripped and the glass fell and the water was spilt. The queen gave orders immediately that the girl's head should be cut off for this trifling offence. She would heed no remonstrance and the sentence was carried out. Almost every day people were being put to death at Ambohipotsy or at Faravohitra for a variety of offences. At the same time whole villages were being subjected to the *tangena*, and many people died under it.

During this time of comparative quiet for the Christians Rev. William Ellis, who had been a missionary of the L.M.S. in the South Seas, made a total of three visits to Madagascar. His first visit was in 1853. He had to remain at Toamasina, his port of disembarkation. The queen sent word that she was too busy to see him, though the tone of her message was cordial enough. He was only able to see a few of the Christians, and he had to take care, for there were enemies of the gospel at Toamasina. The Christians spoke particularly of the shortage of Scriptures. He then returned to Mauritius, and made another visit to Toamasina in the following year. He was still not able to make his way to the capital. The government was afraid of the cholera, which had broken out in Mauritius. On this occasion he was able to bring in about 1500 New Testaments and Scripture portions, which he had to smuggle into the country. He reports as follows: 'As the officers of the custom-house had strict orders to seize all books, my great difficulty was to get them on shore from the ship, as the captain was unfriendly. I could only conceal them in my pockets, or tied under my dress. In this way I generally managed to take eighteen Testaments and other books at a time. I breathed more freely when I had entered my house, locked my door, and deposited my treasure in the innermost room.'[1]

It seems that the government was at this time seeking to re-establish contact with the European powers, which had been largely broken off. William Ellis made a third visit to Madagascar in 1856, and this time he was able to journey to the capital. He was told he could only stay a month, but was cordially welcomed and well treated during his stay. He brought a communication from the British government to the queen, expressing the friendship of Great Britain towards the people of Madagascar. But the real purpose of his visit was to ascertain the situation regarding the Christians. He had been able to send a few books from Mauritius, and these he shared with the Christians. He also had some funds from England which he was able to disburse for the relief of the distresses of some of the believers. He had contact with a number of the leaders of the Christians, but he had to be very circumspect in all his meetings with them. Christianity was still proscribed and he was not able to gratify his wish to attend one of their secret meetings. It would have been too dangerous. William Ellis enquired closely as to the life and general conduct of the Christians and expressed himself well satisfied. For all of twenty years these people had been cut off from outside influence so far as the Christian faith was concerned, but they were evidently taught by the Holy Spirit through the Word of God,

Along the road from Antananarivo to Antsirabe, the little wayside shop is typical of the Malagasy countryside

and he found no evidence of any serious departure from the faith. The Christians made no lists of their numbers or of their places of worship. Should they be arrested or their houses searched no incriminating information would be found.

Soon after William Ellis' departure for England a Frenchman, M. Lambert by name, returned to Madagascar after having tried unsuccessfully, both in England and France, to secure aid to dethrone the queen and set up Rakotondradama in her place. The prince royal was greatly disappointed at the failure to elicit support from these European powers. The conspirators decided to go ahead on their own with the help of M. Lambert. Jean Laborde, another Frenchman, who was much thought of by the queen, was also implicated in the plot. Some few of the Christians were involved in the conspiracy, but the great majority stood aloof and would have nothing to do with it. At the last moment some of the Malagasy nobles got cold feet. When the conspirators came to the palace the gates had not been opened and the plot was not able to proceed.

The queen's wrath knew no bounds. She seems to have thought that the Christians had been implicated in the plot, but the names of very few of them were known to her. She would have put the Frenchmen to death, but feared the consequences of such an act. The queen called a *kabary* for 3 July 1857, in which she intended to proceed against the Christians, and indeed against any of the people whose crimes deserved punishment in her view. Jean Laborde told a companion that it was the most awful *kabary* he had witnessed. Thousands of people fled in terror; some perished from hunger and exposure in the forest, while others were brought back to the city and tortured.

The queen's anger was directed principally against the Christians. But Christianity had become widespread and even many of the nobles and officials were secretly Christians. So, in spite of all the efforts of their enemies, aided by the soldiers, only about 200 were caught. A list of the names of seventy Christians was prepared for the queen. However, the list had to go first to Prince Rakoto, who immediately tore it into pieces.

But the Christians were still hunted with implacable severity. Villages were searched from end to end and if any believers were found the whole village was likely to suffer for having concealed them. In some cases when the soldiers came to a village all the inhabitants had fled. The two Frenchmen and other Europeans who were in the capital at the time were expelled forthwith.

Of the Christians who had been captured fourteen were stoned to death at Fiadanana. This seems to have been the most brutal form of execution the government could think of, with the intention of causing the greatest degree of fear and terror. Their heads were then taken off and fixed on poles. Most of those killed were leaders and pastors in the Christian community. They went to their death without fear, and in the mercy of God their sufferings were not prolonged. Three others were stoned to death soon afterwards. Fifty people were compelled to submit to the *tangena* and eight of them died. Nine of the Christians fled for their lives and escaped, but they suffered considerably in their wanderings. One was sold as a slave. The greatest sufferings were endured by twenty-seven of them who were bound in heavy iron fetters and sent off to parts of the country where fever was rife. Few of these survived. The fetters were put round their neck and feet and several people were bound together in this way. When one died his head had to be taken off to free the body, and then the survivors had to carry his fetters as well as their own. In this way their suffering grew worse and worse until they all died.

This was in many respects the most cruel persecution of all that the Christians had suffered. But it was the last. The believers still needed to exercise great care, but as the queen grew older and weaker in health her severity against the Christians was relaxed. The two princes did all they could to relieve the wants of their brethren and supplied them with clothing, rice and money, until even their ample resources were almost exhausted. Not only the princes, but many of the nobles and officials, themselves believers in their hearts, gave according to their ability for the relief of their fellow Christians.

A cousin of the prince, Ramboasalama, was plotting to take the throne. He had been one of the enemies of the Christians. As the queen's condition grew worse and no efforts by idols, charms or divination could stay the course of her disease, the prince royal was counselled not to leave the palace. The queen died on 16 July 1861 and Rakotondradama was proclaimed king as Radama II.

Closing years of the persecution

This persecuting queen was without doubt an instrument of Satan for the destruction of Christianity in her kingdom. The age-long conflict between the Head of the church and the great adversary was seen in a most virulent form on the island of Madagascar. What hope did these people have, so ill-equipped as they were, to stand against the might of a determined ruler and the powers of a well-organized state? Their numbers were few, they were ill-prepared for the storm which burst upon them, and they had inadequate contact with those best able to help them. But they did have in their own language the Scriptures of the Old and New Testaments, which they prized as their most precious possession. This last was the secret of their endurance and cancelled out the handicaps under which they began. For a period of twenty-six years they were smitten by five waves of persecution. Their leaders were cut down and removed, their books were taken away from them, their places of worship were demolished and they themselves suffered every refinement of cruelty their tormentors could devise. Yet they stood firm. They maintained their position with a firmness that their adversaries could neither gainsay nor resist. Yet in their firmness there was no arrogance, no boastful self-confidence, nor did they ever evince any hatred or anger towards their persecutors. When charged with praying and reading the Scriptures, their reply was, 'Yes,' they had done so. Far from being angry with those who were out to destroy them, they said rather, 'If those who persecute us did but know the blessedness of the love of Christ, they would love him too, instead of destroying those who believe in his name.' It is not surprising then that as a result of their testimony thousands of their fellow Malagasy also came to the point of faith and discipleship and were themselves faithful unto death.

No one will ever know how many Christians died as a result of illness and privations during those twenty-six years. The number could well have exceeded 1000. That was in addition to the 200 or more who were put to death by poison, fire, spear and stones. Yet in spite of all, the little company of about 1000 young and untried believers increased during those years to 7000, and probably more. Persecution had no power to destroy the church of Jesus

Christ. Rather we may say that the church grew because of the trials it endured. Where there is no testing the faith we profess can be lightly held and poorly esteemed. We can walk comfortably with the world. But when the child of God is called upon to renounce his faith or die, then happy is he if he can say, 'We must obey God rather than men,' and act accordingly. When the world confronts the Christian with fire and sword, then there is a special blessing for those who learn to overcome by the blood of the Lamb and the word of their testimony and who love not their lives unto death.

David Griffiths, fellow student and fellow worker with David Jones, had been permitted to remain in Madagascar until almost the year 1835. As he left Antananarivo on his way to the coast he bade farewell to a Malagasy on the road. He held up his New Testament and his Malagasy companion remembered his words as he held the book above his head. 'I have taught you that this is the Word of God,' he said. 'Your queen says it is only the word of man and she will destroy it. But as we believe that this is really the book of him who said, "Heaven and earth will pass away, but my words will never pass away," then all that Ranavalona can do will not destroy it and it will live and grow.' His words had been proved true.

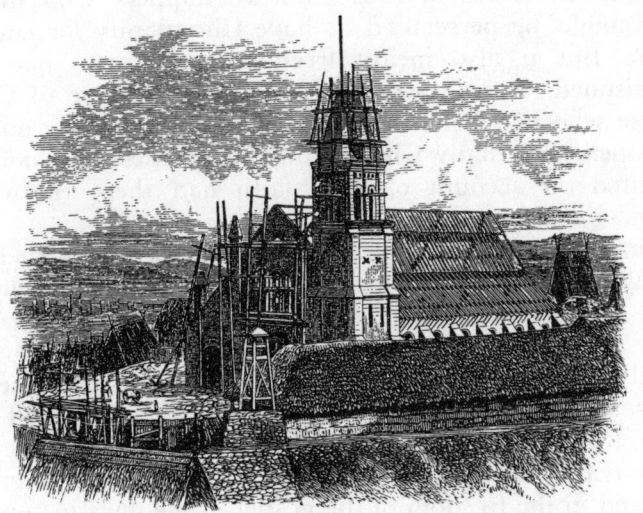
Memorial Church at Ambatonakanga - the first stone church in Madagascar

11.
The sun shines again

The Malagasy refer to the persecution of the church during those years as the *Tany Maizana*, or the time when darkness covered the land. Similarly, the death of the queen and the accession of Radama II introduced the return of the light. The transition from the old queen's reign to the accession of Radama was carried through smoothly. Ramboasalama's ambitions were known and his house was surrounded by troops. He submitted quietly and took the oath of allegiance to the new king.

One of Radama's first acts was to allow everyone to worship as he thought best and to declare that everyone was free to teach and preach the faith he professed. This edict relieved the fears of those idol-worshippers who thought they might be persecuted or have Christianity forced upon them. But it also meant freedom to all who had been imprisoned, banished or enslaved for the name of Christ. Those who had been in hiding were able to come out into the open, and many whose lands and possessions had been forfeited on account of their faith had them restored to them.

But above all, the exiles were now able to return home. Many who had been banished to distant parts and who had been thought dead long since came back to the capital and were reunited with their friends and relatives. We can only faintly imagine the joy of the reunion and at the same time the sense of loss in the realization that other banished loved ones would never return. Some who returned were bed-ridden and came home only to die, but others lived and rejoiced in the freedom of the gospel in the days to come.

The directors of the London Missionary Society had kept a close watch on the situation during the years of persecution. We have already noted the visits of William Ellis to Madagascar during those years. Again in 1861, at the direction of the society, he left England and in the following year proceeded to Madagascar and made his way up to Antananarivo. Before the end of that year a party of missionaries had also arrived. William Ellis had begun to explore the possibility of erecting places of worship as memorials to those who had died in the persecutions. The society agreed to this and Christians in England, including pupils in the Sunday Schools, raised a total of £13,000 for this purpose. It was then necessary to secure the appropriate pieces of land. A Malagasy law forbade the alienation of the land of Madagascar to foreigners, but these buildings were to be for the use of the people themselves. Proper title was secured to the land and arrangements were made to pay compensation to any whose land might have been encroached upon. Four sites were considered appropriate for the erection of the memorial churches. James Sibree came to Madagascar in 1863 to be architect and superintendent of building for the new edifices. It was fitting too that the veteran artisan missionary, James Cameron, who was living in retirement in South Africa, should be recalled to assist in the supervision of the building operations. James Cameron's connection with Madagascar extended from 1826 till his death at the age of seventy-six in 1875. The buildings eventually erected are a tribute to the work of these men and to the Malagasy builders. They are all imposing stone buildings, such as would adorn any city anywhere in the world.

The first memorial church to be erected was at Ambatonakanga, in the lower part of the city. This was the site of the first chapel, the building which was used by the persecuting authorities as a prison to house the Christians. The foundation stone for the new building was laid on 6 January 1864. The Malagasy had never, up to this time, erected a stone building of this size and character, so close supervision was needed at the beginning until the workmen had acquired the necessary skill and experience. The Ambatonakanga church is built on a slope, and is a solid robust structure with a corner belfry tower.

Ambohipotsy was the site where Rasalama had been speared to death in 1837, and Rafaralahy in the following year. The hill of Ambohipotsy (white hill) is the highest point of the city and at the southern end of the elongated rise on which the city stands. It is 500 feet above the surrounding rice fields, and the view from the top extends for miles. Here a beautiful stone church with a tall slender spire commemorates those who died nearby.

Not far from Ambohipotsy is the great stone precipice known as Ampamarinana, the Rock of Hurling, where thirteen Christians were rolled in mats and pushed to their death in 1849. The third memorial church was built on this spot, right at the top of the cliff.

Faravohitra is at the northern end of the town, and is the place where the four nobles were burned at the stake. Here is yet another imposing stone edifice, like the others large enough to accommodate a congregation of several hundred worshippers. Faravohitra is sometimes known as 'the children's church'. It was built with the pennies of British Sunday School children and also commemorates the child who was born in the flames.

A fifth building, erected a little later, though not so large as the others, also qualifies as a memorial church. It is at

Volcanic Lake Itasy

Fiadanana, at the place where fourteen believers were stoned to death in 1857.

These buildings, large as they were, were not adequate to accommodate all who wished to worship, and several other buildings were erected in different parts of the city. A century later Antananarivo gave the impression of being a city of churches. The Amparibe church, where Andriambelo ministered for so many years, was the largest church building in the city, and is the venue for many combined gatherings.

As we have seen, when Queen Ranavalona died in July 1861 she was succeeded by her son Rakotondradama, who took the name of Radama II. Unfortunately his early interest in the Christian faith was not maintained. He came more and more under the influence of the pagans. In 1863 there was a rebellion and many of the king's ministers were seized and imprisoned. He himself was strangled to death by the rebels in May of that year. His last words before he died were 'I have never shed blood.' It seems unlikely, from his words and actions towards the end of his short life, that he had truly been born again. William Ellis knew him well, particularly in that final year, and he said this of him: 'God had raised up this young prince at a most critical period in the early history of the Martyr Church of Madagascar. He gave him influence with his mother which no other human being ever exercised, filled his soul with a horror against the destruction of human life in any form, and warmed his heart with sincere and disinterested sympathy towards all suffering from injustice and cruelty; and he was honoured by the Christians' God to lighten in their favour the heavy iron rule under which they had so long been bowed down. He saved many persons' lives, denounced persecution, established perfect religious liberty, and, while guaranteeing unfettered religious action, had afforded complete legal protection to Christian and heathen. But his destitution of the principles of religious life in his own soul disqualified him for anything closer than a mere external association with the outward progress of Christianity.'[1]

The throne was offered to his widow Rabodo, and she became queen under the name of Rasohérina. The new queen restored the idols and the priests to the position they had occupied during the reign of Ranavalona. This action had at least the effect of quieting the apprehensions of those who thought that Christianity was gaining too much power. However, the queen also showed her goodwill towards the gospel by placing her adopted children with the missionaries to be instructed by them.

The mission was recommenced with great vigour. We saw how a party of missionaries was sent out in 1862, and these were followed by others in quick succession. There was a tremendous work to be done. Many thousands of people, in Imerina and in distant provinces, were in desperate need of Christian instruction. Mr and Mrs Toy were among the first party. Mr Toy gave faithful and valuable service in spite of recurring ill-health until his death at sea on the way home in 1880. Dr Davidson, who arrived with the same party, set up a dispensary which grew in time to a comprehensive medical service for the whole of Imerina. James Sibree returned to England, completed a theological course and came back to render many years of valuable service to the kingdom of God in Madagascar. Mr J. Richardson was sent out as a schoolteacher in 1869, and he did valuable work in that capacity. But his lasting memorial to the work of God in the island is the excellent Malagasy/English dictionary which bears his name.

We saw that the Rev. William Ellis was the first to go up to Antananarivo when the country opened. On his earlier visits to the island he had only had limited communication with the Christians on account of his not knowing the language, but in 1862 he was acting as interpreter for others. He had formerly been a missionary of the L.M.S. in the Society Islands, but in the latter years of his life he gave unstintingly of himself to the Malagasy Christians. He has left full and copious accounts of his journeys to Madagascar. He was a keen observer and has penned some fascinating accounts of the life of the Malagasy people as he saw it in his day, from the queen and her ministers in the palace to the humble peasant. He was still appealing eloquently for Madagascar and its people almost up to the time of his death in 1872.

In the closing pages of his *Martyr Church of Madagascar*, Ellis recounts the spread of the gospel to the surrounding

The sun shines again

country. He tells of the people of the village ofАмпа́рафа́ра́вато on the north side of the capital. He says, 'The whole population of this village had been votaries of the idol or idols kept in the village. But the Gospel had penetrated there, and a number of these villagers had become Christians. Appropriating one of their houses for public worship, they had abandoned the idols, and met together in the house thus set apart for the worship of the true God. Some of these now came to Ambatonakanga, attended our worship, and applied for admission to fellowship with us. Those who knew them having testified to their Christian character, they were baptized and afterwards received into the Church.'[2]

So even the keepers of the idols were abandoning their charges and seeking entry into the Christian church. But neither at this time nor later did Madagascar as a whole abandon the old ways and settle for the Christian gospel. Each generation must accept or reject the gospel message for itself, and in this imperfect world the battle for the souls of men is never entirely won. To this day *sikidy*, *ody* and *fady*, (divination, charms and taboos) still rule in the hearts and lives of many of the people.

What then has been achieved? The gospel came to Madagascar from outside, brought to the country by the European missionaries. Very soon, in the providence of God, missionary support was withdrawn. A faith and a religion alien to Malagasy ways of thinking would soon have withered and died in this situation, and this, of course, was predicted by the enemies of the gospel. But this gospel message answers the deepest need in the heart of man and, furthermore, those who receive it soon find themselves linked by faith to its divine source and are not merely tied to the human instrument. So it came about that very soon the gospel message was deeply implanted in the breasts of multitudes of Malagasy people. The charge has often been made that a people receive and embrace the gospel because of the prestige or benefits which accompany it. The situation in Madagascar gives the lie to such a charge. Those who heard the gospel from the missionaries received it for themselves, and when the missionaries had gone they not only held it fast but they shared it with others. But by that time, humanly speaking, there was all to lose and nothing to gain from becoming a Christian. With the help of the Bible in their own language this was not a second-hand faith, but an essential part of the life of many Malagasy people. And so it is to this present day. From henceforth Christianity must be reckoned with as a force, as an essential element, in the life of the Malagasy people. That is not to say that all Malagasy have become Christians or may be expected to do so. But it does mean that the Christian church has become, and still is, a not insignificant part of the life of Madagascar. David Johns's comment in 1834 that 'This church will continue while the world lasts' may well continue to be true of the Christian church in Madagascar. The one qualification is that that church should remain true to the Bible as the Word of God and adhere to the faith therein proclaimed. This, of course, is true of us all.

12.
The ongoing story

A short final chapter should suffice to bring our story up to date. Queen Rasoherina died in April 1868. She was succeeded by her cousin, who took the name of Ranavalona II. The new queen had already believed the gospel and at her coronation the royal idols were conspicuous by their absence. Emblazoned on banners around the platform were the words 'Glory to God', 'Peace on earth', 'God with us', and so on. Prominently displayed on a table in the sight of all was a copy of the Bible. In the following year, 1869, the queen ordered the destruction of the royal idols. Many of the people also committed their idols to the flames, and many of them no doubt experienced a sense of release as these tokens of the old ways were destroyed. It would be wonderful to be able to relate that that was the end of idolatry in Madagascar, but such was by no means the case. The worship of idols continued on the part of many; charms were still worn; the diviner was still sought after and lucky and unlucky days were still observed. Unhappily these customs often continued alongside a profession of Christianity.

This is, of course, only to emphasize that the reception of the gospel message and the evidence of its transforming power are a matter of the individual heart and conscience. The queen may be baptized into the faith and destroy the idols on which her predecessors had depended; many of her followers may willingly follow her in this, but it does not follow that the same precious faith is found in the hearts of all of them. The subject may feel safer in doing what his ruler does, but his heart may remain unchanged. So it was here: the forms of Christianity were agreed to, but in many instances its content was absent.

None the less there was a real and genuine expansion of the gospel. Reports of those years tell of a tremendous outreach in every direction. One of the missionaries, Mr Sewell, reported, 'My own firm conviction is that, with much that is unsatisfactory, there is a great work going on in this country of which the Holy Spirit is the Author, and that, with much that is merely outside profession, there is a large amount of genuine Christianity which is decidedly on the increase.' This reads like a sober assessment of the situation with the recognition that 'All that glitters is not gold,' but that nevertheless much fine gold was to be found. Mr Jukes, another missionary, writes, 'I am filled with wonder and gratitude at the showers of grace with which God is favouring His Church. Everywhere that I go the cry is for instruction in Divine things, and Christian congregations are being formed in every direction.'

The French government had shown an interest in Madagascar since the seventeenth century and that interest had never waned. A variety of circumstances led to increasing friction between the French and Malagasy governments in the latter part of the nineteenth century. As a result France sent an expeditionary force against Madagascar in December 1894. A French protectorate was imposed in the following year, and in 1896 the French parliament voted to annexe Madagascar as a French colony.

Among other things this annexation had the effect of strengthening the hands of the French Catholic missionaries who were then labouring in Madagascar. They sought to equate, in the minds of the Malagasy, loyalty to France with adherence to the Catholic faith. Much persecution and confusion resulted. One French colonial administrator of this period was an atheist by conviction and also totally opposed to the work of the Protestant mission. Thus from several directions new problems and burdens bore down on the church and the mission. But at the same time the whole island came for the first time under one rule, and many benefits accrued to Madagascar with the advent of a single stable administration. The country was opened up with roads, post and telegraph services and eventually a railway to Tamatave, the name by which Toamasina came to be known.

The church learned to adapt to the new situation and continued to be a major factor in the life of the people. By the middle of the twentieth century some two-fifths of the population owed allegiance to Christ either as Protestants or Roman Catholics. At the same time many less well-developed parts of the country remained still outside the effective reach of the Christian church.

The political situation underwent a further change in 1958, when, as a result of a 'Yes' vote in General de Gaulle's referendum, Madagascar became a separate state within the French community. Full independence was achieved under Philibert Tsiranana on 26 June 1960. Tsiranana became the first president of the independent Malagasy Republic. There has been a shift in emphasis since 1960. Some instability in government, which was not helped by a worsening economic situation, led to resignations, attempted *coups* and an assassination in the higher echelons of government. Madagascar moved further to the left politically. While its foreign policy is officially non-aligned, there are close links with Moscow and Peking. Lt. Commdr. Didier Ratsíraka was sworn in for a seven-year term as president in January 1976, and that term was later extended.

What a variety of administrations the church in Madagascar has had to contend with! First there was Radama's cordial but calculated support, followed by the unremitting hostility of Ranavalona and her advisers. Subsequent Queens of Madagascar alternatively tolerated and actively encouraged the church and the Christian gospel. Under French administration a whole new set of restrictions was imposed, beginning with the requirement that the method of education and the medium of instruction were to be French. Since independence there has been a left-wing government but although it has links with those Eastern Bloc countries whose aim has been the extermination of Christianity within their borders, no such policy has been introduced in Madagascar. Through all these changes the church has continued its work and witness, for while God's people may have to live under a variety of regimes their confidence is not in the prevailing style of government, but in God. Nowhere is this more true than in Madagascar.

An event which took place in 1985 indicates more clearly than many words the power and influence of the Bible and of the church in Madagascar in the 1980s. The year 1985 was the 150th anniversary of the first complete Malagasy Bible. The event was widely celebrated throughout the country. In January of that year a combined service of thanksgiving was held to which the president and other leading national figures were invited. President Ratsíraka gave an address on that occasion, in the course of which he disclosed a considerable knowledge of the Bible and, it may be said, a measure of faith in its teaching. Among other things he is reported to have said, 'If the Bible were a human being it would now be defunct or very old. It is because it is the very Word of God that it is eternal. The Bible has been persecuted in a number of countries. It is those who have persecuted it that are dead, but the Bible remains with more life than ever.' This is by any reckoning a remarkable testimony by a national leader to the place and power of the Bible.

It has been customary for a number of years for government officials to take part in various ceremonies on important public occasions, ceremonies which were related to traditional religious beliefs, ceremonies equivalent in some ways to the ancient custom of displaying the royal idols. The president has said that he will no longer attend such ceremonies.

1987 marks the 150th anniversary of the death of Rasalama, the first martyr for Christ in Madagascar. As Malagasy Christians commemorate this significant event in their national history, they are not giving recognition to a faith which was once held, but has now been superseded. Rather it can be said that the faith which moved in the heart of Rasalama 150 years ago is the same faith which moves with equal power in the hearts of thousands of Malagasy to the present day.

Notes

Chapter 1

1. In fairness it must be mentioned that the account of Dr Phillips' dream rests on evidence which some historians consider to be doubtful. The doctor's dream and their call to Madagascar as a result of it are not referred to by either Jones or Bevan. It is not recorded in the biography of Dr Phillips. However, the arguments against the dream and its results are arguments from silence, except that according to L.M.S. records David Jones was to be appointed to Africa, and only went to Madagascar because another candidate dropped out.

   Is it not possible that both men were moved to enter missionary service as a result of the story narrated by Dr Phillips, even though in the case of one of them it might well have been Africa and not Madagascar? Other students of Dr Phillips, for example, David Griffiths, went into missionary service. The doctor's zeal for the cause of Christ in the lands over the seas is not questioned.

2. The Missionary Society was formed in September 1795. News of William Carey's first six weeks in Bengal stirred the heart of Dr David Bogue of Gosport, who issued a statement in 1794 addressed 'To the Evangelical Dissenters who Practise Infant Baptism'. His 'Appeal' was published in the *Evangelical Magazine*, and this resulted in a group of Anglicans, Methodists, Presbyterians as well as Independents coming together to form 'The Missionary Society'. This new society got on with its task with commendable speed and in the following year the missionary ship the *Duff* sailed for the South Seas with a party of missionaries. In 1818 the name of the society was officially changed to 'The London Missionary Society'. It is now known as the 'Council for World Mission'.

Chapter 2

1. Mervyn Brown, *Madagascar Rediscovered*, 1978, p. 25. Mervyn Brown has a long and interesting section on the arrival of the various peoples in Madagascar.

2. Something of the extent of the Madagascar slave trade may be gauged from figures given in *Madagascar Rediscovered* by Mervyn Brown. He quotes a colonial report dated 1676 which refers to a population of over 32,000 slaves in Barbados from Guinea and Madagascar, and of Malagasy

slaves in Jamaica, the Carolinas and even in Boston. When the British government first began to suppress the slave trade to Mauritius, local planters there maintained that 40,000 new slaves were needed to cultivate the available land. Most of these would have come from Madagascar, and it was this trade which Governor Farquhar was seeking to suppress on behalf of his government. Even in the 1840s there was a clandestine trade in slaves to Arabia and the United States (See Brown, *Madagascar Rediscovered*, p. 178).

Chapter 3
1. Brown, *Madagascar Rediscovered*, p. 144.
2. *L.M.S. Archives*, 18.10.20, quoted by Sonia E. Howe, *The Drama of Madagascar*, p. 162.

Chapter 4
1. Howe, *The Drama of Madagascar*, p. 173.
2. Ludwig Munthe, *La Bible à Madagascar*, p. 133.
3. James Sibree, *The Madagascar Mission*, 1907.
4. J.J. Freeman & D. Johns, *Narrative of the Persecutions of the Christians in Madagascar*, 1840, p. 62.

Chapter 5
1. Brown, *Madagascar Rediscovered*, p. 176.

Chapter 6
1. Munthe, *La Bible à Madagascar, p. 36*.

Chapter 8
1. Brown, *Madagascar Rediscovered*, p. 176.

Chapter 9
1. William Ellis, *Faithful unto Death: The Martyr Church of Madagascar*, p. 165.

Chapter 10
1. Ellis, *Faithful unto Death*, pp. 166–7.

Chapter 11
1. Ellis, *Faithful unto Death*, p. 226.
2. Ellis, *Faithful unto Death*, p. 231.

Glossary

Most Malagasy names of people and places are compounds of ordinary words. Personal names are generally prefixed with 'A' or 'Ra'. Thus 'be' (pronounced *bay*) = big, or great. Ra-be = Mr Big. For places, the prefix 'An-', 'Am-', 'Antan-' etc. signify 'at' or 'at the place of'. In the following list of words the syllables to be accented are marked.

Am-báto-na-kánga (At the guinea-fowl rock). The first place of worship was built at Ambatonakanga, in the city of Antananarivo. This was also the site of the first martyr memorial church.

Am-bódin' An-do-hálo (*am-body [vody]* = at the foot of). The site of one of the early schools, also of a place of worship. This is also in the capital.

Am-pá-ma-rínana The Rock of Hurling. A great outcrop of rock, at the south end of the city, standing some 500 feet above the plain, where thirteen of the Christians were thrown to their death. The ledge onto which they fell is 150 feet below. A memorial church stands on this height.

An-drí-ana Prince or sovereign. The word is also part of the Malagasy name for God, *An-drí-a-má-ni-tra* = Fragrant or enduring Prince. Many proper names begin with Andria-.

An-drí-a-na-mpó-in-imér-ina (1745–1810). The ruler who united the tribes and clans of Imerina, and the father of Radama I. His name means 'Prince of the people of Imerina'.

An-tan-án-arívo The capital of Madagascar, and formerly the capital of the Hova kingdom. The name was shortened by Europeans to Tananarive, but the original name has been restored since independence. The city is near the centre of the island, on a plateau over 3000 feet high, and is built on a long steep hill. This hill is in the middle of a great plain, which is dotted with villages, many of which are themselves on small hills. The whole area in between is covered with a carpet of rice-fields, whose colour varies with the seasons. These surroundings accentuate the height and character of the city, while the view from the city itself is almost unrivalled in its spectacular beauty. Owing to the steepness of the hill many of the streets are steep and narrow, and there are numerous foot-tracks comprising hundreds of steps. The name means 'a city of a thousand', and it is said that when Andrianampoinimerina conquered the city he placed 1000 men in it to inhabit it.

Bé-tsi-léo A tribe and district on the southern end of the central plateau. The gospel seems to have spread to Betsileo next after Imerina.

Hova (pron. 'Hoover') A branch of the Merina people in the centre of the island. It is sometimes used as a name for all the inhabitants of Imerina.

Ka-báry A public proclamation, a message from the sovereign or the rulers; an assembly convened for public business; business or public speeches; an important matter.

Lámba The usual outer garment or shawl worn by most of the people. It is generally a piece of white material worn by the women round the shoulders like a shawl, with one end tossed back over the shoulder.

Lapa, or 'palace'. If our impression is that the Malagasy were a primitive or uncivilized people, then the use of the word 'palace' may seem incongruous. But the early chiefs and kings built for themselves substantial houses of wood. Later palaces were imposing structures of brick and stone, and adorned with artifacts of European origin, or fair

Glossary

imitations of the same. 'Palace' is probably the best English rendering of the Malagasy word *'lapa'*. The Malagasy were apt imitators of European ways. Several Malagasy had been abroad, even before 1835. Malagasy troops were trained in English drill, and many English terms were introduced, most of which are now obsolete. The Malagasy queens and nobles dressed in the height of European fashion and danced the polka. The barbarous and the civilized existed side by side.

Ra-dáma Radama I was the king who welcomed David Jones, the first missionary. He died in 1828. Radama II succeeded the persecuting queen in 1861. He reigned for less than two years and was assassinated.

Ra-bódo Wife of Radama II. She became queen on the death of her husband, and she reigned under the name of Rá-so-hérina.

Ra-fara-lahy (Mr Last Man, or Boy) A fairly common name. Rafaralahy was the second martyr for Christ in Madagascar.

Rá-fara-vávy (*vavy* = female; girl or woman). This lady took the name of Mary at her baptism. From being an ardent idol-worshipper she became a zealous Christian. She escaped to the coast and travelled to England. She died in Mauritius in 1848.

Rana-válona The name of the persecuting queen. She was sometimes called Ranavalo-manjaka, from *'manjaka'* = to rule. Two subsequent queens took the same name. Ranavalona II was a baptized Christian believer. She ordered the destruction of the royal idols in 1869. Ranavalona III was the queen at the time of the French occupation in 1895. She was banished to Algeria, where she died.

Toamasina (also known as *Tamatave*) The principal port on the east coast and the chief point of entry to the Hova kingdom in the centre. The *Rue Jones et Bevan* is a street in Toamasina named after the pioneer missionaries of the L.M.S. The Malagasy are reverting to the Malagasy form of spelling and pronunciation of many well-known places. So the Malagasy 'Toamasina' has been used in this book, though this east coast port was known for most of the time under review as Tamatave.

Tsi-tia-lainga The term means literally 'Not loving falsehood'. It was the name of a silver-headed spear belonging to the government, engraved with the name of the queen and with these words. It was carried, as a mark of authority, when messages of the queen were delivered to the people. The name was then applied to the person carrying the spear.

Chronology of important events

September 1795		The founding of the Missionary Society, afterwards known as the London Missionary Society.
	1797	Birth of David Jones, first missionary to Madagascar, at Neuaddlywd, Wales.
	1818	David Jones and Thomas Bevan arrive in Mauritius and proceed at once to Madagascar for a preliminary survey.
	1820	David Jones returns to Madagascar and proceeds to Antananarivo, the capital of the Imerina region.
	1828	Death of Radama, king of the Merina people and friend of the missionaries.
	1830	First Malagasy New Testament completed and distributed.
	1831	First Christians in Madagascar baptized into the faith and received into the church.
	1835	Christianity declared illegal in Madagascar by Queen Ranavalona. Most of the missionaries leave the country.
14 August 1837		Death of Rasalama, first martyr for Christ in Madagascar.
	1838	Death of Rafaralahy, second martyr for Christ in Madagascar.
	1840	Persecution renewed in Madagascar: nine Christians executed, including Paul the Diviner.

	1841	David Jones dies in Mauritius.
	1849	The Great Persecution: eighteen Christians put to death, while hundreds suffered slavery, banishment, fines or flogging.
	1857	Last outbreak of persecution: fourteen Christians stoned to death.
16 August	1861	Death of Ranavalona, the persecuting queen.
	1896	Madagascar becomes a French colony.
26 June	1960	Madagascar becomes an independent republic.

Bibliography

Articles

Antananarivo Annual, or The Madagascar Magazine. Printed in Antananarivo, on the L.M.S. Press, 1875–1900. Various articles from the issues 1881–1900.
The Life of Andriambelo, as told to the Rev. Thomas Lord. Unpublished manuscript.
'Andriambelo', in Malagasy Magazine *Ny Sakaizan' ny Tanora*, [*Friend of the Young*], May 1964.
Rev. J.T. Hardyman, 'Madagascar's Bible Year', in *The Evangelical Magazine of Wales*, Dec. 1985/Jan. 1986.

Books and Booklets

J.J. Freeman & D. Johns, *A Narrative of the Persecution of the Christians in Madagascar*, John Snow, London, 1840.
Rev. William Ellis, *Three Visits to Madagascar*, John Murray, London, 1858.
Rev. William Ellis, *Madagascar Revisited*, John Murray, London, 1867.
Rev. William Ellis, *Faithful Unto Death: The Martyr Church of Madagascar*, John Snow, London, 1876.
Rev. James Sibree, *The Madagascar Mission*, L.M.S. London, 1907.
Rev. J.T. Hardyman, *Rasalama, the Heroine of Madagascar*, Kemp Hall Press, Oxford, 1937.
Sonia E. Howe, *The Drama of Madagascar*, Methuen & Co. Ltd, London, 1938.

Pastor Rabary, *Ny Maritiora Malagasy [The Malagasy Martyrs]*, F.F.M.A. Press, Antananarivo, Madagascar, 1951.

Joyce Reason, *Storm Over Madagascar*, Eagle Books, London, 1957.

Mme. Marthe Ramiaramanana Ralivao, *A Condensed History of Madagascar*, Lutheran Press, Antananarivo, 1960.

Ludvig Munthe, *La Bible à Madagascar*, Egede Institute, Oslo, 1969.

Rev. J.T. Hardyman, *Malagasy Refugees to Britain*, Université de Madagascar, Département d'Histoire: Nos. 5–6, 1977, Rev. J.T. Hardyman, *The LMS and Madagascar, 1795–1818*, Nos. 7–8, 1978.

Mervyn Brown, *Madagascar Rediscovered*, David Philip, Claremont, South Africa, 1978.